The Journey

ABOUT THE AUTHOR

Arnold M. Patent brings clarity, simplicity and focus to the opportunity for expanding in consciousness and joyfulness. His gift is in supporting those who are willing to ascend from living as limited beings in the human experience into the peace, freedom, abundance and unlimited creativity of life as their true Selves, Divine beings.

After bringing to completion a successful career as an attorney in New York, Arnold began to practice Universal Law. In the eighties and nineties he traveled the world giving hundreds of seminars and forming Mutual Support Groups, many of which still meet today, where thousands of participants feel free to open their hearts and expand their trust in the loving beings they are.

He has been featured on radio, television and in numerous magazines and newspapers. He has authored seven books including bestselling *You Can Have It All,* and most recently *Money* and *The Journey.*

Currently, Arnold leads an ongoing international support group called the Circle of Love and Joyfulness that meets through tele-conference.

Arnold and Selma, his wife of 56 years, along with their two married daughters, each of whom have two children, reside in Los Angeles, California.

He may be contacted through his web site www.arnoldpatent.com.

The *Journey*

REVISED AND
EXPANDED

ARNOLD M. PATENT

Celebration Publishing
Tucson, Arizona

ACKNOWLEDGMENTS

Selma for being the perfect wife, friend and partner

Betty and Frank McElhill for their generous support

*All those who over the years have played with me in
Universal Principles and mutual support, making
our Journeys one of Love and Joyfulness*

*Kaelin Chappell Broaddus for enhancing the
spirit of the book with her designs*

CONTENTS

Seeing Clearly

The Journey Continues

INTRODUCTION

I have spent the last 30 years trying to understand the game we call *life*. The process began with the insights that came as I sought to clarify what had been so confusing.

After sharing these insights informally with friends and acquaintances, I was invited to present them on a more formal basis, first in living rooms and then in larger public venues. Many of the details of the early years of this experience are contained in my first book, *You Can Have It All*.

Staying conscious of these insights, or using the always-available distractions to divert my attention is my choice. I have noticed that as I heighten my awareness, the insights multiply as well as the support to more deeply accept and appreciate the process. My awe of the way I am being supported encourages me to deepen my commitment to continue. I am grateful that my commitment to expand my awareness is always matched by an increase in the level of support offered to me. This support took the form of one-on-one coaching.

I have kept extensive handwritten notes of the coaching experience knowing that one day I would report these experiences in a book. One morning I awoke to the realization that I could best tell the story by giving the reader as much information as possible including my personal experiences. Appreciating how enjoyable this approach would be for me, I could not wait to begin.

When I wrote "The Journey" in 2002, I was four years into a coaching process that lasted four more years. The expansion of consciousness from this intense process led me to create a teleconference-based Circle of Love. Started in 2007, this ongoing program encourages participants to free them Selves of self-created limitations. This revised edition is a way to share the additional insights and expanded awareness gained since the first printing.

The
Journey
Begins

CHAPTER 1

❦

A New Perspective

ONENESS

I am One with everything. The words are simple and straightforward. Yet, the attempt to fully grasp the concept remained elusive for many years. When I was ready to gain clarity, the reasons for avoiding the concept became clear.

Who wants to be one with poverty, crime, disease and terrorism? Who wants to be one with fear, anger, frustration, depression and shame? As a practical matter, I was not ready to begin to accept the concept of Oneness, or any of the other Universal Principles, until I was willing to recognize, at least intellectually, that these disagreeable conditions and uncomfortable feelings are based on how I see them and what I call them.

THE IMPORTANCE OF OUR PERSPECTIVE

The gap between the natural state of the Universe and the way the world in which we live appears to us seems insurmountable until we see the true relationship between them. Instead of being far apart, these states are very closely related. In fact, they are just different phases of a continuing journey.

The journey begins when, as our Soul Self, all that we know is our true state of being. Our experience is only of harmony, peace, unconditional love and infinite abundance. Aligned with the unconditional love, support and peaceful Power of the Divine, we allow all aspects of the Divine to manifest through us as our perfect experience—being the God Presence. Eager to re-experience our natural way of being, the Soul Self initiates an exploration of our human journey.

INTENTIONAL AMNESIA

In order for this exploration to be meaningful, we have to give up memory of who we really are, and what our natural state is. There is no way that we can accept feeling helpless, angry or mean-spirited if we retain awareness of being the God Presence.

IT TAKES THE GOD PRESENCE

Who other than the God Presence (our Soul Self) could possibly give a sense of reality to the complex illusions we have imagined: Hitler and Mother Theresa; atomic bombs and peace marches; anger and forgiveness; retaliation and acceptance.

We have given our Selves many lifetimes of extraordinary experiences. During this time, awareness has expanded for many people and with it their perspective. Some are now ready to enter the next phase of our journey.

CHAPTER 2

⮂

Two Phases—
An Introduction

PHASE ONE

For simplicity sake, we can divide our lifetime into two phases. The first phase encompasses the period during which we cleverly disguise the flow of Divine Power through us by filling our consciousness with beliefs that life is challenging and limited making it seem that:

1. we are at the effect of events and circumstances, and

2. the Universe and all in It are often our uncaring nemeses rather than our loving supporters.

This is the phase during which our participation in these events and circumstances justify feelings we call fear, pain, grief, loss and abandonment. Although we often wish this phase would disappear, like a bad dream, it contains valuable information for the next phase of our journey: a description of how we divert and resist the flow of Divine Power through us.

In the absence of surrendering to and aligning with this flow of Power, we continue to experience the reflection of the beliefs that we planted in our consciousness. Interfering with the flow takes great effort. The Power is enormous and is constantly pushing its way toward freedom. Much of the discomfort we feel is the pressure of this internal conflict.

Why Resist the Power

We resist the free flow of the Power so that we can explore life as opposite to our natural state. This is the other side of the coin of giving up memory of who we really are. And both are prerequisites for the creation of our journey as human beings.

Hiding Our Power

With the support and guidance of our Soul Self, we hide our resistance to this Power in the very places we are determined to avoid—situations, beliefs and feelings that we find uncomfortable and distasteful, such as failure, illness, fear and shame. Our Soul Self then ensures that we keep the Power hidden by installing a gatekeeper that we can call the Protector. The mission given this part of us is to do whatever it takes to keep us away from this Power.

The Protector is diligent and resourceful. Every time we get close to the Power, this guardian of the hiding places finds a way to send us elsewhere. From many years of experience, the Protector knows the most effective ways to misdirect us. Memory lapses, self-doubt and avoidance of discomfort are just some of the patterns that the Protector relies on to carry out the mission assigned to It.

PHASE TWO

Freeing the Power

When we begin the process of looking for the Power, we need to be mindful of the strategies we have employed to deter us. However, we cannot treat these strategies as obstacles to overcome. Rather, we utilize these same strategies to find the Power.

Seeing part of us as creating obstacles for other parts keeps alive the feeling of inner conflict that was one of the strategies we employed to keep the Power hidden. The approach that works for me is creating harmony within, bringing all parts of me together in support of my new intention.

I create this harmony by acknowledging and appreciating the parts of me that have brilliantly hidden this Power and keep me away from it so that I can have the experiences I have come here to have. In other words, I see the creation of apparent conflict within me as purposeful. Then, I focus on the fact that I am not really at conflict with my Self; I have created the illusion of conflict.

Our Soul is always aware of who we really are. The challenge we face is accepting that truth and having it become real for us. We are seeking to bring the Soul's awareness into our human awareness.

As we build our acknowledgment and appreciation for what it takes to resist and avoid this Power, we are verifying for our Selves that our intention to proceed is real. We are also demonstrating to the Protector that we have truly changed our intention from one of avoiding and resisting this Power to that of surrendering to and aligning with It. As soon as that intention reaches 100%, the Protector becomes our ally in supporting us in surrendering to and aligning with the Power.

CHAPTER 3

⟳

Getting Ready

INTENTION

In order to understand the presence of any current experience, we first look at universal mathematics. This is mathematics in its simplest form. All that we need to remember is 0% and 100%. Anything less than 100% equals 0%.

Whatever situation we are facing is present because our intention to have that precise experience is 100%. When we look to have another present experience, our intention to do so must first reach 100%. Otherwise, no movement occurs.

LOVING OURSELVES

Everything I experience is colored by the way I feel about my Self. When I feel less than unconditionally loving and accepting of my Self, I see and feel the world around me in the same way. This is true since I am the whole of the Universe, and there is nothing outside of me.

How I feel about my Self is determined by my beliefs. As a way of providing me with the best possible support, the Universe makes certain that every belief I hold is reflected back to me as though I am surrounded by 360 degrees of mirrors. I am always seeing and feeling a reflection of the state of my own consciousness. I am constantly living the drama that is the playing out of my beliefs.

This is a huge gift that the Universe presents to me. Accepting this gift means a willingness to acknowledge that every opinion I hold, anger I express, and circumstance I find repugnant is the way I see or feel about my Self.

A common belief and one that I accepted is that I am not perfect just the way I am. As long as I hold that belief, I cannot possibly love my Self unconditionally. Until I love my Self unconditionally just the way I am, I cloud my view of the unconditional love and support of God, my primary and core relationship.

POWER

One of the central themes of the book is how we relate to, use and experience power. So, what is power, where does it come from, how do we use it and what happens when we do?

There is only one true Power in the Universe—Divine Power—used exclusively by God. That Power, unconditional love, the sole energy in the Universe, is what we are, what surrounds us and flows though us all of the time.

Although as humans we cannot access this Power, God has created a derivative power for us to play with. That derivative is the illusion of power. Therefore, whatever we create with that power is an illusion. This gives us the freedom to explore using that derivative power any way we wish without fear of causing harm to ourselves, or anyone we are playing with. In order for our creations to seem real, we forget that the power we are using isn't real.

The vehicle we use to play with the power is a belief.

BELIEFS

Each of us is the Power and Presence of God: all-knowing and all-powerful. At the deepest level of your being, the Soul level, you know who you are. You create beliefs to disguise that truth. The repetition of beliefs makes them seem real and they become patterns of behavior.

A belief is a feeling attached to a thought. The feeling gives the thought its power making the thought seem more real than your knowing.

The belief resides in your consciousness. Divine Power, unconditional love, flows continuously from the Divine through your consciousness activating whatever beliefs you have placed there. The activation creates a physical representation of the belief.

Again, a belief is a feeling attached to a thought. The feeling quality determines what manifests. When the thought and the feeling are in conflict, the feeling controls.

How you are feeling is determined by how you see the world in each **now** moment. How you see the world is determined by the illusions you have created from the beliefs you are holding in consciousness.

JOYFULNESS

In order to maintain a belief, you are diverting the flow of Divine Power (unconditional love) through you into derivative power. When you open the energy in a belief, you feel the unconditional love that the Divine is constantly showering upon you. The feeling quality of unconditional love is joyfulness.

Remember, nothing you create is real. Everything is fluid, as are your feelings. You know how rapidly your feelings change and how rapidly what you are experiencing changes in accordance with the change in feelings.

You can set the intention to raise your level of joyfulness and expand the time you are able to maintain your level of joyfulness. This will bring to your attention the beliefs you are ready to open so that you feel more joyful.

You place the value on everything in your life. You tend to value things you feel good about higher than things that induce worry, fear, frustration and the like. The times when the events and circumstances in your life are unsettled and disorderly, and you are feeling uncomfortable, are times to treasure and feel good about. What you are experiencing is the process of reconfiguration of the events and circumstances to a higher level set in motion by your expanding consciousness.

Appreciating everything in your life, particularly the times that are unsettling and uncomfortable, is a big step toward having a consistently joyful life.

In order to create a belief, you must have full intention to disguise who you really are. Opening the energy in the belief requires an equal amount of intention. With that intention in place, remind your Self that you installed the belief in your consciousness so that you can have your human experiences. Then, remind your Self who you really are, and in that expanded state and with heart wide open, embrace the belief and all aspects of the situation in unconditional love.

Repeat this exercise until all that is left is the love that the belief was disguising. You will notice that the belief has no more importance to you.

NON-JUDGMENT

I know the Principle of non-judgment: Whenever I judge anyone or anything, my experience with that person or situation remains the way I see it. The release of the judgment frees the energy so that I may expand my view of the person or situation.

When what I see or feel seems less than perfect, I know I have located a judgment.

A judgment is a belief. Use the same process to free the love held in your judgments.

When the judgment involves a person, embrace that person in your open heart until you become one with that person. The amount of love you free by using this process is beyond description. You will appreciate the beauty of the process after you have had the experience of allowing more unconditional love into your awareness.

With the love flowing through you, envision a whole new way of relating to the person or the situation. This creates a more expanded way of playing in the human, more in alignment with the joyfulness of being who you really are.

Finally, doing this process by your Self is challenging. Doing it with the unconditional love and support of like-minded individuals is much less challenging and becomes fun and exhilarating. The gain of each becomes the gain of all. The Circle of Love and Joyfulness is designed for that purpose.

NOTHING OUTSIDE OURSELVES

I pay close attention to any situation that causes me discomfort, since I know I have located a place where I am diverting or resisting the flow of Power through me. This focus supports me in opening the energy in the beliefs that I am not perfect just the way I am, and that there are events and circumstances that I have created to disguise the love. Examples of energy I have opened are beliefs in the reality of disease, failure, shame, deceit, pain, working for a living and death. Opening the energy in these beliefs is a way I expand my capacity to appreciate that I am the whole of the Universe and that there is nothing outside of me.

OUR EMOTIONS

Love is the only energy in the Universe and joy is the only true feeling. Fear, shame, distrust and anger are names we have given to feelings to help us disguise the joyfulness. We use the events in our lives to deepen these emotions, creating additional layers of separation between our human Selves and the free flow of unconditional love through us. This also creates a greater distance between our human Selves and our joyfulness.

When we revisit these places for the purpose of releasing the joyfulness, we remove the labels we have placed on the energies. They are, when free of the labels we have assigned to them, a broad array of feeling qualities. The range of these feelings is no different from the vast pallet of colors available to an artist, or the infinite variety of harmonics available to a composer. These feelings are the God Presence—an indescribable richness and the forever expanding beauty of joy.

The
Phases

CHAPTER 4

つ

Phase I

Let's look at our lives as though we are characters in a play. This play is written before we are born under the guidance of our Soul Self. Each individual play is part of a larger play and each role is crafted to be in support of all other roles.

Each participant is a volunteer who knows that all the support that is needed to play the role is provided in advance. At this formative stage, every participant knows who he really is and what it takes to have the play seem like a real experience.

We know the perfect family, culture, community, events and circumstances that will give us the experiences we choose to have. We know the beliefs to create that support us in resisting or diverting our access to the Divine Power of unconditional love so that the play follows the script.

With our Soul Self's support, we proceed to create beliefs that dissuade us from accessing the Power; and, we assign a part of our Selves the role of Protector with the assignment to do whatever it takes to block our access.

The play continues with the building of the illusion of how powerless we are, and how much we are at the effect of forces in the world around us. We accept the reality of such illusions as struggle, danger and failure. We funnel feelings into these beliefs creating intense emotional states such as fear, anger and shame, which serve to keep us away from the places where we can access the Power of unconditional love.

We tell our Selves that we are not acceptable just the way we are, and set up conditions we must comply with, such as working hard and pleasing others, before we are entitled to feel good about our Selves. We also learn to interpret expressions such as anger, fear and shame as devoid of love. These conditions and interpretations become additional ways to avoid opening to and accepting the Power.

CHAPTER 5

∽

Phase II

PART ONE

The awakening begins:

The awareness emerges that there is more to life than struggle and pain, and that we are not as helpless as we once thought.

Our hearts open more.

The Universe begins to appear as a loving and supportive Presence.

We start to feel the flow of Divine Power through us and less at the effect of forces outside of our Selves.

We see life less as adversarial and competitive and more as mutually supportive.

The contrast between how we are accustomed to see the world and the new way it appears becomes more obvious.

We find our Selves fluctuating between these two worlds and not totally comfortable in either.

As we expand our trust in this new way, we notice that there is a part of us that resists our forward movement; the more deeply we try to trust, the harder it becomes for us to do so. The Protector is still doing what we have instructed it to do.

This leads us to the awareness that in order to enroll support for our new vision, we must first convince the Protector we are truly committed to do whatever we must to accept who we really are, and what we know the Universe really is. The next phase of the journey is about to begin.

PART TWO

The awakening continues:

The beliefs that support our limited view of life become more evident, as they present them Selves in our daily activities.

We realize we have set up very powerful mechanisms to keep the limited view in place.

We enroll the Protector's support to help us open the energy in the beliefs that keep limitation in place.

We see more of our lives as a reflection of what we believe.

We begin to recognize that everything we experience is information we can use to expand our awareness of how perfectly we have created what we are experiencing.

We appreciate how the Power of unconditional love manifests through us, limited only by our acceptance of limitations that we have created.

We focus on expanding the flow of unconditional love through us.

We encourage the emergence of our Soul Self.

What our Soul Self knows:

Joy, abundance, peace, harmony, gratitude, generosity, creativity and inspiration are all aspects of our natural state of unconditional love.

Our purpose is experiencing and expressing the Power and Presence of God in ways that bring us the greatest joy.

We exercise this power in our imaginations. Our physical world, a brilliant creation, exists only in our imagination: a world of make-believe that we convince our Selves is real.

Nothing in our physical world has any power.

There are no mistakes or accidents.

We are perfect in every situation just the way we are.

Everything keeps expanding: the intensity of anger; the richness of abundance.

Abundance is infinite and unconditional; we accept and appreciate as much as we wish.

The more we savor and deeply appreciate each moment, the more moments we find to savor and appreciate. This is a way to enjoy and expand our natural state of abundance.

We are all volunteers who have a specific role to play in each other's lives. We are all perfectly prepared for our roles.

Every event is an accurate reflection of the state of our consciousness. These events reveal beliefs that make it seem that we are separate from Divine Power. The more committed we are to uncovering these beliefs, the more support the Universe provides to see them clearly.

Each of us is the whole of the Universe.

Each of us is the Power and Presence of God, and we are all One.

When we fully accept this truth, our lives become a joyful game.

Abundance

CHAPTER 6

⋑

What is Abundance?

Abundance is our natural state—the unconditional love and support of the Universe flowing freely through us at all times and all circumstances. The perception that we are not abundant—making the opposite of what is true seem real—has taken the fullness of our creative power. Over many years we have committed our Selves to create beliefs that lack is real. Using our creative power to open these beliefs requires the same level of commitment.

One of the ways we open to the flow of abundance is to appreciate what we already have. Appreciating something increases its value. Conversely, failure to appreciate something diminishes its value. The more deeply we appreciate what we already have, the more fully we open to the abundance that is already flowing through us.

This brings us to the Principle of Giving and Receiving: we give knowing that we already have—that the abundance of the Universe is always flowing through us. As we open the beliefs that have hidden this truth, we become aware that:

Giving and receiving are always in balance and reflect the consciousness of the giver. When the giving is motivated by a desire to express generosity and appreciation for the gift of abundance that has already been received, the vacuum created is filled with more abundance.

When the giving is motivated by obligation, the vacuum created is filled with a greater sense of obligation. When the giving derives from a sense of lack, the vacuum created is filled with a greater sense of lack.

Since most people carry beliefs in obligation and lack that they created in Phase One, that consciousness mandates their experience. Opening beliefs in obligation and lack require a deep commitment together with the guidance of someone who has achieved the desired consciousness, as well as a setting of mutual support that mirrors the Oneness that is the Universe, a communal energy that embraces all in unconditional love.

When we open our Selves to feel the truth that each of us is the All, we realize that we are giving to our Self. That is when the Principle becomes real.

We enjoy as much as we are willing to appreciate. This is how we enrich our lives.

Since everything is love, we know that whatever appears as less than love is a disguise we have created. By embracing the disguise in our fully open heart, we allow the energy hidden in the disguise to be experienced as the unconditional love it has always been.

Once we have opened to the flow of love within us, we are ready to expand our enjoyment of that love by expressing it in ways that are most natural to us: doing what we love for the pure joy of the experience. As we open to more of the flow of love through us, we do what we love in new and ever-expanding ways.

As we commit our Selves to do more of what we love, it is helpful to keep the following in our awareness:

We are all imbued with the full power of the Universe to express in our own unique ways what we love to do, for the pure joy of the experience. This is a gift from the Universe.

26

All of us are provided with the perfect support to live life abundantly.

Each of us is whole and complete and nothing can be taken from us.

Fully and freely doing what we love is an expression of appreciation to the Universe for the gift of that talent.

We are all equal.

The Universe and all in It are constantly showering us with love and support.

What we love to do is a talent that brings us joy when we fully and freely express it. Joining with others whose talents complement ours creates an expanded energy that transforms the interaction into a whole new way of playing together.

We can free the power hidden in our beliefs, expand our appreciation for who we really are, and do what we love more easily and enthusiastically by joining with others in mutual support.

CHAPTER 7

Opening to the Flow of Power

Since much of the Power you are seeking to release is embedded in matters that you least wish to appreciate, such as health issues, financial problems, emotional discomfort and disharmony in relationships, it is helpful to remind your Self to:

appreciate that the Universe keeps bringing you to where you have hidden the flow of Power;

stay in the feeling quality of the hidden Power just the way it is, no matter how uncomfortable the feeling;

accept that the more uncomfortable the feeling, the more Power you have located;

let go of any description you have of the Power such as fear, shame, anger or discouragement;

open your heart and embrace the fullness of the Power no matter how uncomfortable you feel, continuing with this process until the energy is experienced as the love that it really is;

feel appreciation for all participants in the drama;

feel appreciation for the Universe in bringing you this gift;

feel appreciation for your Self for accepting the gift;

feel appreciation that the Power of the Divine is always flowing through you;

feel and see everyone as the Power and Presence of God.

CHAPTER 8

∽

Avoiding Abundance

LIMITATION

Creating the concept of limitation is a brilliant way to avoid enjoying our natural state of abundance. I chose to explore this concept in many ways. One way in particular seems worth sharing—paying less for something is better than paying more.

I did not fully appreciate the extent to which I had resisted the flow of abundance until I started the process of opening the energy in my many beliefs in limitation. That is when I realized that by limiting what I am willing to give, I am also limiting what I am willing to receive. Giving and receiving are always in balance. Knowing that there is no limit to the flow of abundance, I now receive gratefully and give generously. (See meditation entitled, "You Are Like a Creek Bed" page 118.)

CONDITIONALITY

Our lives are filled with conditions. We created the belief that unless we meet these conditions, love and support is withheld from us. First at home, then at school and finally in the workplace, we trained our

Selves to behave in prescribed ways so that we are accepted, and avoid unpleasant consequences.

Complying with conditions diminishes our freedom to express our Selves, and our talents for the joy of doing what we love. Complying with conditions serves to resist the natural flow of abundance in all aspects of our lives.

Accepting abundance as our natural state means:

1. paying attention to the conditions we believe to be true as they surface;

2. reminding our Selves that our acceptance of these conditions is intentional and purposeful;

3. embracing the conditions, and our Selves for accepting them, as the way to free the energy hidden in the conditions;

4. allowing the freed-up energy to flow through us as the abundance that it really is.

CHAPTER 9

❧

The Present Moment

A Law of the Universe is that everything occurs in the present moment. Thus, the full Power of the Universe flows through us as the God Presence in each present moment.

We have created many ways to divert our attention from the constant flow of this Power. The main way we do this is by making it seem that what we are experiencing is separate from and exists outside of us.

Until we accept and appreciate that everything we experience is within our consciousness, an illusion created by our beliefs, we deal with our world as a nemesis rather than an opportunity to explore a wide variety of experiences.

What determines how much freedom we have to see the world in a new way is how much importance and power we give to what we are seeing and experiencing. Remove the importance and power and what we see becomes the soft, gentle, and peaceful energy of love.

The only energy in the Universe is unconditional love—the Power of the Divine—that flows through our consciousness manifesting for us whatever we believe. As we open the energy in our beliefs, the manifestations become closer to our natural state as a reflection of the Divine.

This can only be done in the present moment by fully appreciating the creative process we have used to convince our Selves that something can be separate from us, and a power outside of us.

Diverting our attention from the present moment is a way we disconnect our Selves from the flow of this Divine Power that contains within it the infinite abundance of the Universe. We can only open to and receive that abundance with our undivided attention and full appreciation. This is a lot easier said than done. That is why I maintain a constant focus there.

A related Principle is that everything is perfect just the way it is. Another way of describing this is that we are always seeing an exact reflection in the physical of what we hold in our consciousness. Putting the two Principles together, we have the perfection of what is, just the way it is, in each present moment. Next come the acceptance, appreciation and practice of these truths.

Let's look at an aspect of my life as an example. I grew up with the belief that I needed to create and accumulate investment income in order to maintain a comfortable lifestyle when I chose to retire, or was forced to do so by ill health or other unforeseen events or circumstances. I also believed that advanced age brought inevitable physical decline and therefore accumulating assets was the best way to prepare for that eventuality.

Of course, holding those beliefs ensure they become a self-fulfilling prophecy. After unburdening myself of these beliefs, I was ready to free the flow of abundance that my accumulation had retarded. Knowing that holding onto money slows the flow, I keep it moving. And, the flow is abundant.

The truth is that right now my life is just fine. The beliefs that I needed to accumulate funds for the time when I am no longer productive, or wish to retire, or to meet some unforeseen emergency did provide reasons why a financial projection based on future needs would disclose that everything is not fine.

However, having released the beliefs and projections, and accepted what is as perfect, it has become perfect. This approach also reminds me that I am free to choose to see everything that occurs as perfect, just the way it is, and, with my heart fully open, accept each moment as a gift from the Universe.

When what I see initially seems less than perfect, I open to a broader view, that of my Soul Self. From this vantage point I remember that the Universe loves and supports me unconditionally. I remind myself that I am free to receive as much of this love and support as I am willing to appreciate.

Projecting my present circumstances into the future is just a brilliant way to divert my attention from the present moment and thus limit the flow of abundance through me. I know that my embrace of these projections frees the energy in them so they can infuse my talents with new levels of enthusiasm and inspiration as well as opening my consciousness to allow more of the abundance of the Universe to flow through me.

Why should I project what I have now as a future experience? Why should I be satisfied having more of what is present when my creative power can create far beyond my present situation?

The real fun in life, that which brings me great joy and fulfillment, is joining with others in exploring whole new ways of enjoying the unlimited abundance that is awaiting my readiness to receive. A way to prepare to receive these unlimited gifts is by inspiring each other to keep expanding in consciousness.

The state of my consciousness determines the amount of abundance I allow to flow through me from the Divine. Emptying my consciousness of the beliefs I have created to make limitation a way of life is my choice and my opportunity.

Was I really concerned about not having enough?.

No. My concern was about the shame of not meeting a standard originally set by the culture in which I grew up, but that I had adopted as my own.

In directing my attention to the feelings of shame and fear of failure (illusions I had created), the Universe offered me a gift: showing me places where I had hidden the illusion of power. I accepted the gift by reminding my Self that what I have been calling shame and fear of failure are just disguises for my Power as a God Presence.

After much practice, I have come to appreciate that failure is just a belief created in my vivid imagination. I know that I only see failure reflected from others as long as that belief is present in me. And if I do, the Universe is giving me the gift of showing me where I still have the illusion of power hidden.

SUMMARY

Your world is your creation. The energy of this creation is the flow of Divine Power through the filter of the beliefs you hold in consciousness.

You conjure up these beliefs in your imagination and the resultant dramas exist solely in your vivid and fertile imagination. These dramas can only be illusions since the power of the Divine remains within the Divine at all times and under all circumstances. Your use of the energy that comes from the Divine is devoid of any real power.

Everything you experience is completely within you, and exactly as you perceive it: a game you are playing with other players who are just aspects of yourself.

Although these dramas seem real, they are illusions made to seem real by vesting them with power, also an illusion.

Playing with your creations as real reinforces their reality and the reality of the beliefs that lie behind them.

The new game is:

retracing the steps that have given the illusions a sense of reality as you keep your focus, in each present moment, on the flow of Divine Power through you;

surrendering to the flow of Divine Power through you. (See chapter 11, section entitled, Trust in the Abundance for the process);

reminding your Self that your physical world is an illusion created by the flow of Divine Power through the beliefs held in your consciousness;

trusting that all Power in the Universe is unconditional love no matter how it appears;

seeing unconditional love everywhere and in everyone;

feeling gratitude for the gift of the Divine Power constantly flowing through you;

knowing that each belief you release opens you wider to the flow of Divine Power that manifests in the physical more in alignment with your natural state as a Divine being, and

enjoying the richness and beauty of your divinely created world, just the way it is, in each present moment.

↭

CHAPTER 10

Perceptual Reality and the Mirror Principle

Abundance is present in my life. The same is true of harmony, peace, freedom and joy. Fear, shame and limitation are disguises I create in my consciousness (imagination) to cloud the view of my true Presence.

The Mirror Principle and state of consciousness go together. I am always looking at a reflection of my own consciousness. If I believe in limitation of any sort, I see that limitation reflected back to me in my daily life.

When I believe in lack, I fail to appreciate all the abundance present in my life. Appreciating what I have increases its value. This expands my present abundance.

Seeing evidence of abundance everywhere is simple. There is so much that we take for granted. Building a consciousness that is filled with appreciation attracts more to appreciate.

Appreciating what I have encourages me to be generous. That, in turn, encourages others to be generous to me.

Our society is built on the concept that wanting more improves life for everyone. The truth is that wanting more is evidence of the belief in lack and the absence of appreciation for what we presently have.

Wanting more has encouraged those with the greatest appetites for more to create a society with ever-growing disparities of wealth and recurring cycles of boom and bust. (See meditation entitled "Appreciation" page 117.)

Feeling appreciation for what I have is natural to me, as is being generous. Training myself to believe that lack is real has required great intention; opening the energy in that belief has required equal intention.

The Mirror Principle was the constant reminder of my acceptance of beliefs that the Universe was not abundant; that I was not talented and enthusiastic about expressing my talent; and, that I was not loved unconditionally by all. When I perceived any of these conditions to be true, the circumstances in my life appeared to back me up. I knew that I was free to make a case for anything that I chose to believe.

The approach I now use is to keep in consciousness how abundant the Universe is, and how talented I and everyone I interact with is. If I see anyone who appears less than that, I know I have not fully accepted the truth of who I am. For, I cannot see in another something that is not present in my consciousness.

It is helpful to remember that we live our lives in accordance with agreements we make before we come here. All that we need to live that way is given to us. Being homeless is not a sign of failure. Being a millionaire is not a sign of success. These are just personas we create. We remain Divine Beings exploring ways to live in the human.

I am committed to be present in each moment of my life and to accept that moment as perfect just the way it is. In this way, I expand my awareness and experience of the absolute abundance that is present in my life. The more I open to each present moment and embrace it as a wonderful gift, the more magnificent that moment becomes, the more energized I feel, and the more open I am to accept the limitless abundance of our loving and supportive Universe. I also eagerly share these gifts.

CHAPTER 11

Opening to Abundance

DOING WHAT WE LOVE AND
ACCEPTANCE OF ABUNDANCE

Each of us has at least one talent—something we love to express—for the sheer joy of the expression. Also, each of us has a personality profile that is divinely designed to complement other personality types. When talents and profiles are harmoniously combined, a new and expanded energy is created.

The joining is a divinely inspired communal experience that mirrors the Universe—the Grand Communal Experience. Oneness is our common purpose. The Universe's purpose for us is to direct us to Oneness.

Each of our talents is unique and a gift from the Universe. Joining together in expressing our talents is our way of appreciating the receipt of the gifts and completes the circular flow of the energy from the Universe through us and back to the Universe through those who enjoy the expression of our talents: from the All to All.

The Power that flows through us energizes and inspires the expression of the talent in whole new ways. Keeping in mind the Universe's purpose for us—to direct us to Oneness—we align with that purpose as we explore whole new ways of doing what we love. The more we surrender to the flow of Divine Power, the more we replace our conscious-mind attempts to override Infinite Intelligence with ideas we have about what is best for us.

No matter our brilliance, Infinite Intelligence has the benefit of seeing all possibilities from which to choose the best one for us. Surrendering to that Intelligence, while the obvious intellectual choice, is not one we choose emotionally.

My experience is that achieving actual surrender requires joining with others who have set that intention and made that commitment. When the intention and commitment are present, the guidance to support the intention appears.

In Phase One, we create beliefs that Divine Power is dangerous and destructive, making us fearful of going near the Power. The surrender process requires the willingness to embrace this fear in unconditional love until it opens into the true nature of that power: gentle and peaceful.

There is no better way to encourage the flow of that Power than by creatively expressing our talents, in harmony with others, for the sheer joy of generously sharing our gifts. This is our way of demonstrating appreciation for these gifts.

Joining with others whose talents complement ours creates an expanded energy that transforms the interaction into a whole new way of playing together. I see this as our new way of being in business: one that is infinitely joyful, abundant and creative for all involved.

Every talent, whether it be mothering, engineering, painting, composing, cooking or designing—to name a few—when expressed as a joint and complementary activity has the potential to be experienced as a business, a new and fun way of playing together.

TRUST IN THE ABUNDANCE

The richness, the fullness and the Power of the love and support of the Universe are all incorporated in what we refer to as abundance. Living in this abundance is completely natural to us, and is a gift from the Universe for us to accept, appreciate and then share generously. This is our true support.

Placing our trust in the abundance means recognizing that true Power does not belong to each of us. True Power emanates from the Divine and manifests through us.

As for the manifestations, they are all neutral. One is not better than another and all are of no importance. There is no power in any manifestation. All power remains in the flow of Divine Power through us. The more we surrender to this Divine Power, the easier it is to rest in the Power of the process and to see and feel the beauty of the Divine in all manifestations.

As humans we create the belief that each of us has real power and that our creations belong to each of us. In this illusory state of separation from the Divine, we alternate between assuming the role of creator in one moment and becoming the victim of that creation in a later moment.

Having set up conditions for our qualification as Divine Beings, we have made believe that we are cut off from our Divine birthright. The opportunity we have is to support each other in accepting and appreciating who we really are, opening the energy in our beliefs in limitation and conditions, and re-connecting at the feeling level with the extraordinary Power flowing through us. We know we are connected when we are feeling joyful.

Remember, this is not a personal power; this is a Divine Power that is a gift we accept by surrendering to and aligning with as it flows freely through us.

The more deeply we surrender to the wisdom of the Divine, the more readily we see and feel our Selves, and those we interact with, as the Power and Presence of God.

In truth, we are always who we really are, love is always present, and all of our feelings are joyful. There is beauty in all manifestations.

Seeing other than beauty and feeling other than joyful means we are still holding onto beliefs that we are separate from all that is; we are overriding the Divine Power of all possibility flowing through us with the illusion that we have personal power. When we are in this consciousness, we feel the Self-created sense of separation from the Divine and fear from the illusion of aloneness.

ABUNDANCE IS A GIFT

What does accepting abundance really mean? The answer is the willingness to see everything in our lives as a gift of unconditional love and support flowing to us and through us from the Universe. The conditions we place on these gifts are the ways we avoid accepting the flow of this unconditional love and support. Whatever transpires during the day that we do not consider a gift—a beautiful manifestation from the flow of Divine Power through us, and a reason to feel joyful—is evidence that we are holding onto conditions and are thus resisting the flow of abundance.

Another aspect of accepting abundance is determining the value of the gifts we have received. The value we place on these gifts is a measure of the value we place on our Selves, as well as a measure of the amount of richness we are willing to receive.

There is no limit to our value or the richness of abundance available to us. Together we can support each other in accepting an ever-increasing flow of abundance. There is also no limit on how much fun we can have in playing together in mutual support and generously sharing our abundance.

Seeing
Clearly

CHAPTER 12

⊘

Accepting the Gifts

Everything I see and feel is a reflection of the state of my consciousness, and I determine the state of my consciousness. When what I see is limited in any way, I can be certain I have placed a belief in my consciousness. I can also remove that belief.

In order to remove the belief, I must heighten my awareness of what I am seeing and feeling, so that I see and feel clearly what is going on in my life. With that clarity, I know what belief I am holding and can proceed to free my consciousness of that belief.

The opportunity to free a belief is a gift from the Universe. Accepting this gift is up to me.

Why would anyone overlook or avoid this gift? The answer is simple and obvious. Much of what we see is uncomfortable, and we believe that looking at it more closely, and feeling it more deeply will add to our discomfort.

This is proof of how brilliantly we not only distance our Selves from the Power of love and support that is flowing through us, but also maintain that sense of distance. However, the same brilliance is available to us in removing the sense of separation as we open our

Selves to the Power. That brilliant part of us is our Soul Self, the part that sees clearly what is being reflected in the events of our day.

When I expressed my willingness to open to this level of support, the Universe has continuously provided, in the form of intermediaries who hear and see with clarity, the information my Soul Self is communicating to me. There is no limit to the unconditional love, support and abundance that the Universe offers us. There is also no limit to how much of this unconditional love, support and abundance we can accept, appreciate and share.

PROGRESS

Every time I open a belief, I am free from the sense of limitation contained in the belief, and I am now present in a new reality. We do not regress to positions that we have outgrown. What may seem like a fallback is just the return of what is left of the belief for further opening.

Every time I open a belief, I feel more peacefulness, harmony, abundance and joy—my Soul's natural state sitting under layers of beliefs I purposely accepted as the first part of my journey into the human experience. I know that this opening process is a progression from living in the human as a human experience to living in the human as a Soul experience.

KNOWING

The beliefs I have intentionally and purposefully accepted as true become the lens through which I see life. I am not only accustomed to this way of seeing—I rely on it. I have accepted beliefs that some behaviors are good and others are bad, that viruses cause illnesses, and that some people are strong and others are weak.

As I proceed on my journey to open these beliefs, I exercise great patience and perseverance. I know of my wholeness, completeness and the Divine Power flowing through me. I also know that the Universe is unconditionally loving and supportive at all times and under all circumstances. Maintaining this knowing is the way I stay committed to continue with the process of opening to the Divine Being I really am.

BELIEFS AND KNOWING

Our conscious minds use our creativity to make up beliefs that give rise to the circumstances we have come into the human to explore. When we are ready to open these beliefs, our Souls guide us through the process, selecting the ones we are ready to open. The discomforts we feel are evidence of the beliefs we have not yet opened.

Every opening of a belief brings us closer to our knowing, which is our consciousness free of the sense of limitation contained in our beliefs. As stated previously, we do not retreat to positions we have outgrown. Once we open a belief, our greater clarity becomes a new platform from which we move to even greater clarity and knowing.

Our natural state is a consciousness free of beliefs: a state of total freedom, joy, abundance, harmony and peace. *That state is always present, patiently awaiting our full acceptance and appreciation.*

CHAPTER 13

☙

Removing the Veils

EVENTS AND CIRCUMSTANCES

In Phase One, the events and circumstances of our lives are contrivances we use to support us in engaging in the experiences we came here to explore. In Phase Two, they lead us to the beliefs we hold in consciousness that make it seem we are separate from the flow of Divine Power through us. Other than as vehicles for the above-stated purposes, these events and circumstances are of no importance.

When we attempt to make an event or circumstance more to our liking, such as earning more money or finding a more comfortable employment, we are, in effect, trying to change the mirror so that it reflects a more satisfactory image. The image we see is a perfect reflection of a belief we have created to give something the illusion of importance: the opportunity to explore that circumstance or event as though it is real. By using the mirror to guide us in opening beliefs, the same events and circumstances, seen without the veil of the beliefs, appear as unimportant and perfect just the way they are.

REFLECTIONS

Each of us is in perfect support of all others. We offer this perfect support by reflecting accurately the state of consciousness of those with whom we interact. We are all volunteers; no one is a victim or a perpetrator.

Horrific and seemingly unjustifiable acts are wake-up calls to deep truths that we are ready to face: no one really dies; we are each whole and complete and nothing can be taken from us; we are all part of one experience; we are each having the precise experience we have come into the human to have; and most important of all—love is the only energy in the Universe. Whenever we see other than love, our vision is clouded by a belief. The dramatic event is the reminder that we can see with greater clarity when we release the belief that obscures the love.

LOVING OURSELVES UNCONDITIONALLY

I project the beliefs I have about my Self upon the world. Opening these beliefs allows me to see with greater clarity who I really am and thus to feel more love for my Self.

The reasons I give my Self for not being worthy of unconditional love are all beliefs that I have intentionally created and accepted. The closets in my mind are filled with these reasons. I can quickly find justification for withholding love from my Self. I can just as quickly open to greater acceptance and love for my Self just the way I am. (Just the way I am is who I really am—the Power and Presence of God.)

SELF-VALIDATION

Self-validation means accepting, appreciating and loving my Self unconditionally as whole and complete just the way I am. The signal that I have not reached that place is when I look for someone or something for validation. Seeking awards, recognition and endorsements are examples of attempts I have used to fill the void of Self-acceptance and Self-love.

Only I can validate my Self. The Universe in Its infinite wisdom and constant love and support for me keeps reminding me of the presence of this void as a way of encouraging me to fill it. There is no greater gift I can grant my Self than opening my heart to feel this love for my Self.

THERE IS NOTHING OUTSIDE OF US

This is such an important concept that I am calling attention to it once again. Many of the beliefs I held in my consciousness related to events, people and substances that had the capacity to bring me harm, take something from me or bring me pain: viruses, terrorists and economic conditions, to name but a few on a seemingly endless list.

The creation and acceptance of these beliefs is what I came here to experience. However, that was just the first part of my journey into the human. The next part was opening these beliefs so that I returned to the knowing that I am a God Presence, whole and complete just the way I am from whom nothing can be taken.

Removing the veil that clouds the view of our God Presence is seeing and feeling through our open hearts. When our hearts are open, we know:

All is unconditional love;

We are whole and complete;

Nothing can be taken from us;

Giving and receiving love from the fullness of who we are is our natural way of relating;

There is no limit to how generously we can give that love or how much gratitude we can feel when we receive it;

The gratitude we feel is really for the Divine—the Source of unconditional love.

EMOTIONS AS DISGUISES

To re-cap: There is one energy in the Universe and that is love. The feeling quality of love is joyfulness. When what you feel seems other than joyful, you have created a disguise to hide the joyfulness.

There are many feeling qualities (emotions), such as: *guilt, shame, sadness, grief, frustration, anger, resentment, hopelessness, helplessness and abandonment.* There is another feeling quality that has moved to the forefront based on recent events: terrorist activity, environmental disasters and financial disintegration. That feeling quality is *fear.* The response is a desire to protect your Self.

The dangerous events are all perceived as outside of you. Yet, there is nothing *out there.* Everything you experience is in your imagination.

The same is true for your emotional responses. There is no *other* to be angry at, feel sadness for, or feel abandoned by. You, a Divine Being, are the whole of the Universe: Everything is happening within you. And, it is all in your vivid imagination.

When you feel *fear,* or any other emotion, take a moment to re-mind your Self who you really are and that there is nothing *out there.* As for what you are really feeling, there is only one feeling quality that is real—joyfulness—the feeling quality of the only energy in the Universe—unconditional love.

A VISION OF REALITY

Beyond your physical presence is your true entity, the God Presence in all its Divine glory. The power, beauty, magnificence, joy and abundance of this Presence awaits your full recognition, acceptance and appreciation. Take a few minutes to close your eyes and visualize this Presence. Feel the richness and fullness of this Presence. Use this vision and feeling as your new point of reference for who you are. See and feel the events and circumstances of your life as a game you, as a God Presence, came here to play and enjoy. See the participants in this game as your support to remember who you really are. And have fun!

The
Journey
Continues

❧

CHAPTER 14

⊷

Playing the Game

Each of us has created, to some extent, the belief that pain, aging and working for a living are a normal part of life.

Viewed from the broader perspective presented in previous chapters, we can see that each of these concepts is a collection of beliefs that are perfect disguises for Divine Power. By examining these beliefs, we gain appreciation for the extraordinary accomplishment of disguising that Power so that we can have the experiences that seem so real to us.

PAIN

Pain is a great disguise for the Power. Since opening the energy in a belief requires us to feel the energy we have hidden, labeling something as pain is an ingenious way to make certain we avoid going near that hiding place.

The first step in approaching pain is being clear that this characterization of the energy is something we have cleverly contrived. We are responding to the label, which is not what the energy really is. All energy is love—the Power and Presence of God.

After being clear on the first step, make a list of your personal beliefs about pain. Then, taking one belief at a time, review the earlier chapters while keeping that belief in mind. This will heighten your awareness to the reflections you are receiving that tell you how that belief is clouding your acceptance of the truth that you are the Power and Presence of God.

Every thought, action, feeling, event and circumstance in your life tells you what you believe. The opportunity you have is to remind your Self that you are the creator of what you are experiencing, and then to feel appreciation for your creative brilliance.

Do not underestimate the effectiveness of your beliefs in convincing you that you are separate from the flow of Divine Power. Opening the energy in your beliefs takes a great deal of intention backed up by a strong commitment. This will attract the guidance you require to lead you through the opening process.

AGING

Our acceptance of this concept is reinforced daily as we watch people age and then die. Many of us look to postpone aging by exercise and using products that we hope will retard or reverse the process. This approach is similar to the use of drugs to dull or eliminate the symptom of pain. In both of these examples we are looking to something outside of us for help. There is nothing wrong with this. Do whatever feels most supportive. If you wish to open the energy in your beliefs about aging, follow the suggestions given for pain.

WORKING FOR A LIVING

Disguising the truth that abundance is the natural state of the Universe and your natural state is not easy. Your determined acceptance of the concept of "working for a living" is a tribute to your creativity, ingenuity and commitment to make it seem that you really are separate from your natural state.

We are beings not doings. Our lives don't work or not work.

Your appreciation for being who you are—the Power and Presence of God—helps you open the energy around the belief that you are required to do something to be the fullness of who you are.

In preparing to open the belief in "working for a living," it is helpful to remember that you have available all of the creativity, ingenuity and commitment that you used to create the belief. If you wish to open the energy in the belief that you must "work for a living," follow the suggestions given above. This will prepare you to replace the belief in "working for a living" with the joy of doing what you love.

CHAPTER 15

⤎⤏

My Own Experiences

As mentioned previously, we all have gone to great lengths to resist, retard and divert the flow of Divine Power so that we can explore our lives as human beings. Five personal examples illustrate ways I have done this, as well as the ways I continue to free the flow of Divine Power through me.

GRATITUDE

We are all naturally grateful for the love and support that is constantly showered upon us by the Universe and all in It. Feeling gratitude for the events and circumstances I feel good about is easy. However, feeling gratitude for events and circumstances I don't feel good about is something I avoided for many years.

After becoming aware that everything I experience is a remarkable creation made possible by the flow of Divine Power through me, I began feeling gratitude for how resourceful I had been in avoiding this opportunity to feel gratitude.

As the Power and Presence of God, I am all heart, filled with unconditional love and appreciation. By continually heightening my awareness and acceptance of this truth, I am able to easily bring my creations into my heart and embrace them in unconditional love. Having opened my Self to feel more gratitude, I realize that I have also opened wider to the flow of Divine love and the countless gifts that love contains.

I know that my relationship with the Divine is a two-way street. The more I honor the Divine, the more the Divine honors me in return. As I expand my feeling of gratitude for all that I have received, I prepare to receive more.

GENEROSITY

We all have a natural desire to be generous. As I heightened my awareness to ways I was withholding my generosity, I located beliefs I created to keep me away from that source of Power. Many of these beliefs reflected a basic inner conflict: fear of being successful as showing too much Power, and fear of not being successful and therefore not meeting cultural and family expectations. Other related beliefs included: having to work hard to earn anything worthwhile, and having to conserve what I earn to support my wife and my Self in later years. These beliefs reinforced a general belief in limitation and made feeling generous difficult for me.

In addition to opening the energy in these beliefs, I felt appreciation for my Self for how cleverly I had hidden my feelings of generosity. This served to both deepen my feelings of generosity along with my feelings of gratitude.

I gained great appreciation for how committed I had been to stretch the bounds of believability and drama that characterize life as a human being. This deepened my feelings of appreciation for my creative imagination.

OBLIGATION

When I looked at the concept of obligation, I saw the great lengths I had to go to hide the enormous power contained in my natural feelings of generosity and gratitude. The beliefs related to obligation that

I created were so numerous and pervasive, I felt the challenge of embracing them as my creations. These included family obligations such as those demanded of parents to children, spouses to each other, children to parents and to teachers. Then there were obligations to law enforcement officials as well as the obligation to pay taxes.

I accepted these beliefs. I took on a huge sense of obligation to comply with family expectations as a child—by being an excellent student who made his parents proud all the way to becoming a lawyer. I have been meticulously law abiding, and served time in the army to meet governmental obligations.

Perceiving my compliance in all of these instances as involuntary and burdensome, I built up a great deal of resentment toward my parents, the educational establishment and the government. After many years under the burden of these feelings, I spent many years opening the energy around the beliefs that led to these feelings. My current relationship with family members is one of deepening appreciation for the joy and richness they add to my life; and with governments is one of appreciating the many ways they provide support that only government can provide. I express my appreciation in the form of taxes.

There is another aspect of obligation that is worth mentioning— the concept of debt. This is a mirror of our obligation consciousness. The size of these debts is indicative of the amount of power we have hidden in this concept. (Our individual, corporate and government debt has grown to trillions of dollars.)

I participated in this vast endeavor by taking on various debts from personal and business loans to personal and business mortgages. As part of accepting the belief in debts, I used as my model the behavior of the so-called financial sophisticate—the person who borrows money to make more money.

After spending many years feeling the discomfort of playing the debt game in this way, I now enjoy the simplicity and ease of having little or no debts. This is not because having debts is bad or wrong. Borrowing money can be a fun experience, provided it is done with appreciation—enjoying the giving and receiving of a loving energy.

The pervasiveness of obligation and debt as a burdensome experience makes it very easy to find places to practice feeling gratitude for the ingenuity and dedication to hide so much power in these concepts. I continue with this practice in support of opening the immense amount of power hidden in whatever residue of beliefs in obligation and debt remain in my consciousness. I also feel compassion for those still burdened by accepting beliefs in debt and obligation as real.

I also remember that the belief in making money is a brilliant illusion I created. I then open wider to the infinite abundance always flowing through me.

SEPTEMBER 11, 2001

At ten minutes before 8 A.M. PDT on that date, I received a telephone call from an aunt in Connecticut asking me if I heard the news. I said that I hadn't turned on the television or the radio since I awoke. She told me that the World Trade Center buildings were no longer standing, having been hit by planes hijacked by terrorists. I thanked her for the call, related the news to my wife, and we both viewed the replay of the events on television. While I watched, I felt an impact of the energy that appeared to be destruction, devastation and death. As I took those labels off, I resonated with the explosive nature of the energy that kept expanding within me. I had the sensation of soaring like a large bird whose wings were being pushed upward by an enormous flow of loving energy. My heart was filled with gratitude for being the recipient of this wonderful gift.

Listening to the comments of newscasters about the horrendous consequences of the actions of the hijackers, I felt enveloped by the power of the love that had been released in the Universe. Before this event, I was clear that no one dies, there are no victims, and each of us has the precise experiences we have come to the human to have.

However, I quickly became aware that not many years ago, my beliefs included the acceptance of the reality of victims, death and grief. I felt compassion for those whose present experience was not unlike what had been my own. I also saw each of them as the God Presence courageously entering into the fullness of the experiences they came here to have.

THERE IS NOTHING OUTSIDE OF ME

This has been one of the most challenging of the Principles for me to embrace, since I had hidden a lot of power in playing the role of "victim" in many ways for many years. A number of years ago I had two opportunities to test my willingness to accept the truth of this Principle that I wish to share.

On a morning in April of 1999, I was awakened by an uncomfortable sensation on the right side of my chest. An inspection revealed the presence of lesions starting at the midline on the front and continuing around to the spine on my back. I was told I had contracted what is commonly called "the shingles." The medical term is post-herpetic syndrome, a condition believed to be the result of damage caused by a reawakening of the virus that originally causes chicken pox.

The pain was very intense. First, I tried homeopathic remedies, to no avail. This was followed by an analgesic, with the same result. Several people told me that the pain would probably leave after about two months. I decided to tough it out for that period of time. However, no decrease in the pain level occurred. I realized that it was time for me to see the circumstance as perfect just the way it was.

With the support of my spiritual coach, I began the process of changing my description of what I was experiencing from that of being at the effect of forces outside of me to being the force. This meant feeling the fullness of the energy as the Power and Presence of God. This was an enormous challenge since my mind insisted on calling the energy "pain." I continued with this process for over two years before my new description of the energy started to become real for me and the "pain" started to diminish. The "pain" took another couple of years to diminish to the level of discomfort.

In retrospect, I know how valuable the experience has been. I learned the depth of my commitment to uncover the disguises that hide the Power as well as the depth of that Power. I also learned that I am able to trust the truth of how much Power flows through me even though my experience seemed different from that truth.

In the spring of 2001, I noticed termite droppings in two places around my home. I was surprised to again see a reflection of the belief that something can cause me damage. Then I realized that the droppings were a gift. The gift was the information that although I had opened a lot of energy in the belief that something (a virus) can cause me harm, there was a residue of the belief left.

This led to another gift, the opportunity to reinforce the knowing that I am the Power and Presence of God to whom no harm can come. I felt deep appreciation for the support brought by the termites. Since there is nothing outside of me, this is feeling deep appreciation for my creative power.

CHAPTER 16

~☙~

Further Reflections

THE ILLUSION OF CONFLICT

The two most noticeable and common responses to the events of the morning of September 11, 2001 are:

a) compassionate reaching out to the families of those whose physical lives ended as a result of the hijackings, and

b) anger leading to a desire for retaliation against those who supported the hijackers.

The energy in both responses is the same even though they appear on the surface to be vastly different. For there is one energy in the Universe—unconditional love—and that is all we are ever experiencing.

The opportunity we have, as we continue on this human journey, is to expand our vision to keep discovering love until all we experience and express is unconditional love and support. The challenging or fun part, depending upon how we view it, is feeling love for those people who disguise their actions in ways that seduce us into judging them. To simplify the process, remember that this is all taking place in your imagination. The retaliation can only be directed to you.

PEACE

Although the anger and desire for retaliation has led to aggressive action, there is also a surge in the desire to have this event lead to peace. The Universal Principle of Means and Ends tells us that the action and the outcome are one. In other words, when we choose to wage war to bring about peace, we end up with more war. The only way we create more peace is by choosing peaceful means.

For those who prefer the challenge of aggressive activities for the excitement it provides, let's compare alternative approaches. There are two parallel continuums: one is the boredom—excitement continuum; the other is the peace—inspiration continuum.

The reason that many people seek the excitement of aggressive activities is that they are looking to overcome boredom. However, when this choice is made, the excitement must continually increase to overcome the boredom that grows at the same rate. This is true since the Universe is in a constant state of expansion. Whatever choice we make, we keep experiencing more of that choice.

What happens when the choice is more peacefulness? Peacefulness is the absence of inner conflict. Inner conflict arises from the choice to make it seem we are separate from the flow of Divine Power; we set up a tension between the part of us that is naturally peaceful, that chooses to surrender into the arms of the Divine, and the part that chooses to make decisions as though we know better than the Divine how to manage our lives. The result is the creation of the boredom—excitement continuum.

As long as we keep the sense of separation from the Divine alive, the natural expansion of energy causes the tension to build, intensifying our sense of boredom and thus a craving for more excitement.

When we choose inner peacefulness, we encourage a rise in the level of divinely-guided inspiration. Unlike excitement, which generates tiredness from the effort to avoid or resist our natural state, inspiration induces an increased flow of energy. The expression of this energy (love) contributes to greater feelings of peacefulness that in turn stimulate more inspiration.

FREE WILL

The Universe has gifted all of us free will. There are no bad or wrong choices, just an exploration into what happens when we substitute our own intelligence for that of Divine Intelligence. This is all happening in our imagination.

Whatever beliefs we create result in some form of limitation; we become the victim of our creation. We are always free to choose to surrender to the Divine and experience the joy of unconditional love and support.

When we witness in another person an act that appears to be unkind or unloving, we know we are seeing a reflection of a belief we still hold in our own consciousness. We can choose to feel compassion for the person keeping the belief alive as we ask the Divine to heal the misperception in our consciousness. When we have opened all the energy held in the belief, we see and feel only love.

A REMARKABLE ACCOMPLISHMENT

Our vantage point is always the present state of our consciousness—what we really believe. When we proceed to open these beliefs, we often feel uncomfortable. This is because we intentionally encase many of these beliefs in disagreeable feelings so that we avoid going near them—a very clever device we use to keep us from connecting with the joy hidden in the belief.

However, we feel discomfort only because we have taught our Selves to believe the energy we have hidden is uncomfortable. In truth, all energy is love and the feeling quality of love is joyfulness. The process of clearing our consciousness of beliefs that distract us from being fully present in the free flow of unconditional love through us has been set forth in this book. A wonderful way to prepare your Self for embarking on this process is by feeling deep love and appreciation for your Self for the remarkable accomplishment of creating the precise life you are living. And remember, each of us is the Power and Presence of God experiencing and expressing in his/her own unique and perfect way.

THE GREATEST GIFT

The greatest gift the Universe can possibly give us is the opportunity to love unconditionally and to feel that love as joyfulness. Each of us has been offered this gift. As part of our brilliant plan to disguise the truth of who we are, we create beliefs in the reality of conditions that make it seem almost impossible to even consider accepting the gift: shame, failure, disease and death, to name just a few.

When we are ready to allow the truth of who we are, our Soul Self, to emerge, we begin seeing the conditions as disguises for the love and the joyfulness. As our awareness of who we really are grows, so does our appreciation for the value of this extraordinary gift.

Another exceptional gift we are offered by the Universe is the opportunity to see everything as a reflection of the state of our consciousness. This incredibly accurate feedback, that is always available, allows us to see clearly the beliefs we still accept as reasons to avoid loving our Selves unconditionally and expanding our feelings of joyfulness.

This game we call life is set up for all of us to win the ultimate prize—the opportunity to live a life of ever-expanding joyfulness creating whole new ways of playing together. The Universe has offered us this gift unconditionally. This means we are deemed worthy of receiving it by being precisely who we are, just the way we are. When we deem ourselves as deserving as the Universe already does, we claim the prize. And we encourage all others to claim the prize by loving them unconditionally just the way they are.

CLARITY WITH RELATIONSHIPS

In order to love unconditionally, follow this sequence:

1. The first relationship is the one you have with God—being clear that God loves you unconditionally at all times and under all circumstances. This frees you to surrender to God—to all possibility—to align with the surrender and then to rest in the power of that process, which is God manifesting through you. Knowing that the manifestation is perfect, you feel the joy of your natural state flowing through you.

2. Your second relationship is with your Self and derives from the first relationship. When you know you are unconditionally loved and supported by God—the Universe—at all times and under all circumstances, you love your Self the same way.

3. This prepares you for your relationship with others—loving them unconditionally at all times and under all circumstances. You cannot love another more than you love your Self.

4. Love is indivisible: if you withhold love from anyone, you withhold it from everyone.

5. Aligning with this sequence allows you to see your Self and others as who you really are: the Power and Presence of God eager to surrender to all possibility. When you hold this Truth in your consciousness that is what is reflected to you. If you see something else, deepen your surrender to the Truth.

A NEW VANTAGE POINT

There is a way I have found to expand my level of joyfulness as well as my appreciation for the beauty and magnificence of my human experience: view the events and circumstances of my day from ever-higher vantage points, eventually reaching the vantage point seen by an astronaut circling the earth.

The higher my position, the broader is my perspective. Details that at ground level seem harsh and disturbing fade away leaving only the harmony and beauty that reflect the sole energy that underlies all creations—unconditional love.

The details are disguises I have created to hide and separate me from the power in love (harmony and beauty). The disguises have never been real, just evidence of my active imagination.

THE STRETCH

The opportunity you have as a Phase Two player is to experience life in the human as a Divine Being, no longer limited by physicality. There is a technique that you can use to bring you closer to that freedom.

The technique is the stretch. The first part is letting go, in consciousness, of attachment to anything in the physical including all of your physical resources and possessions. This allows you to feel gratitude for the flow of love from the Divine that you have used to create your physical environment.

Having created the belief that money, and the power you have vested in it, is the vehicle used to acquire physical possessions, money becomes a perfect vehicle for the stretch.

You know that money has no inherent power. Creating the illusion of power is a masterful accomplishment. You can feel grateful for the many comforts you have created with money. However, money can be used in a more expansive and natural way: a vehicle for the expression of appreciation. Money loves to flow as an expression of appreciation.

This re-introduces the concept of appreciation, the second part of the stretch. When something appreciates it grows in value. When you express appreciation for something you give it more value.

Expressing appreciation, like love, is natural to you. As with love, your capacity to express appreciation has no limit. In fact, the more appreciation you express, the more you stimulate an inflow of that value-creating force. Also, giving as an expression of appreciation creates a vacuum for more to come in. Receiving gratefully encourages others to give to you that, in turn, activates an inflow to them.

Since you are the whole of the Universe, whenever you express appreciation for another you are increasing your perception of your own value. Since you always receive a reflection of how much you value your Self, the greater your appreciation for your Self, the more you inspire others to value you more, and to value them Selves more.

In Phase One, you use every device available to diminish your appreciation for your Self. In Phase Two, you use every device available to expand your appreciation for your Self.

CHAPTER 17

⋑

The Communal Experience and the Oneness

It is during our early years, as described in the chapters about Phase One, that we create the beliefs that become the judgments that determine the way our lives unfold. As adults, we continue to see the world through the eyes of Our Child.

Our Child carries the weight of these beliefs (judgments) until we free the energy held in them. It is through this process that we learn unconditional love and non-judgment.

Every belief we hold represents a way we have made a limitation about our world seem real. These limitations represent judgments that darken the light emanating from the Divine that knows only unconditional love and acceptance under all circumstances.

Our Child waits patiently for us to play the role of the Divine and demonstrate unconditional love and acceptance, freeing Our Child to bring the purity, innocence, spontaneity and inspired creativity into full and free expression.

Thus, Our Child becomes an adult in our place.

Our role in this process is singular: demonstrate unconditional love and acceptance of everyone and everything under every circumstance. This is how we convince our little ones that they are truly loved and accepted unconditionally. This is how our little ones feel safe to grow into adulthood as their true Selves.

This is also how unconditional love and acceptance transforms from an intellectual concept into a way of life.

Life is a communal experience. Mutual support is natural to us. We give knowing we have it all so that we can receive even more. This is the way we learn what abundance is. This is the way we know Principle. This is the way we free our Divine Selves to play the game that is natural to them.

Our capacity to be unconditionally loving and supportive is unlimited. The more of that we express, the more pours into us to not only replenish but to expand that divinely provided endowment.

We are ready to join together to support and encourage each other to play in our sandboxes as the joyful, spontaneous, innocent and inspired children who know only unconditional love and acceptance under all circumstances.

ONENESS

Oneness is our common purpose. The Universe's purpose for us is to direct us to Oneness.

Divine Power, the Source of life, flows through us energizing whatever beliefs we place in our consciousness. In Phase One we create beliefs that resist, avoid and divert the flow of Divine Power away from the Oneness. In Phase Two we open the energy hidden in our beliefs and align with the flow of Divine Power toward the Oneness.

THE COMMUNAL EXPERIENCE

"It takes a village to raise a child." "We are in this together." "I am my brother's keeper" are sayings that are inspired by the common purpose that connects us even though we think and act as though we are separate. There are many ways to correct this misperception. A simple beginning is to practice seeing our day-to-day activities in the context of a communal experience.

THE SAFE HARBOR

There is one aspect present in the communal experience of life that is essential for us to connect to: the caring, kind and affectionate guidance of fathers and mothers for their children all during their lives.

However, this is hidden under a general misperception that when children reach a certain age, they are capable of making decisions about career and relationships on their own. The truth is that there is no time in the life of a son or daughter that the connection to parents is outgrown. That connection is one of the underpinnings of a successful and fulfilling life that includes career and intimate relationships.

Furthermore, young adults need the guidance that comes from the wisdom gained by parents from their life experiences. This guidance brings clarity to young adults as they face a confusing and constantly changing world. Listening to each other with the caring and affection that each naturally has for the other forms the basis for a life that is rich and fulfilling for parents and children. There is no time when this mutually supportive exchange is outgrown or no longer needed.

In the case of a daughter and a son, the absence of the guidance that connection to their mother and father provides leaves them unable to fulfill the role of a loving and caring partner to their mates.

There is an even more compelling reason to keep this connection strong: there is a deep desire on all parties for this connection. Mothers suffer when they do not have this desire fulfilled; however, fathers suffer the most when their essential function as guides and protectors of daughters is not fulfilled. Fathers do not realize how much they hurt them Selves, how much their essential beingness becomes diminished when they abandon their role as loving and caring guides and protectors of their daughters.

In the absence of fathers fulfilling their roles, mothers encourage their daughters to become liberated independent women because men are disappointing. Until men step up and assume their true roles as affectionate, caring guides and protectors for their daughters, there will be no growth in the creation of intact families as the core of community.

Again, parents have a deep and unending desire to fulfill their roles as loving and caring guides and protectors of their daughters and sons. When they are not functioning in these roles that are definable, important, appreciated and most of all natural to them, they are deadening a desire that will not die. Also, in the absence of fulfillment of this desire, parents will continue to cause pain and hardship not only for them Selves, but for their children and the people with whom their children partner.

The deadening of this desire affects all aspects of a parent's life. This is true since the desire for love and support that emanates from the Divine underlies all desire.

The consciousness of a person who fails to assume the role of a responsible parent to his/her children reveals a lack of maturity that often shows up in the parent's general behavior as more suitable to an adolescent than a mature adult.

When parents do not meet the need for this continuing connection, the son or daughter will often seek someone to fill this need even though the chosen partner is unable to do so. The attempts to fill that need continue and cause stress and discomfort for everyone involved. In the absence of that connection to parents, sons and daughters are less able to fulfill the roles of father and mother to their children.

As for those who are not married, having a safe harbor frees the flow of love in all relationships, prepares the way for a mate if the desire is present, and provides the opportunity for a satisfying and fulfilling career.

If your upbringing was devoid of love and support, or even abusive, know that the love of parents for you is still present, and the desire to express that love is just being held in abeyance. Lest you judge a parent for this behavior, remember you created this Phase One experience. And you made your Self the victim, intentionally.

As the creator, connect with the love hidden in the behavior you are judging and open your Self to the loving relationship that is awaiting your acknowledgement and acceptance.

As for guidance from parents who are set in their ways and seem unable to provide the guidance you desire, they have to reflect your consciousness. When you are able to see them as the Divine beings they really are, the guidance and support will emerge. They have always wanted the best for you. Are you willing to open your Self enough to receive all this love and support?

ESSENCE AND ROLES

Reconnection to your safe harbor gives you the opportunity to achieve a life that is fulfilling in all aspects. However, there is confusion about who is capable of being your safe harbor.

Our society has expanded parenting to almost anyone who chooses to play that role. Emphasis is placed on how well or badly that role is played. Even though there is general acceptance of this approach, it is a complete misperception.

What is being missed is the unique and irreplaceable function of the birth parents.

They are not only agents for the creation of a new being, they are also agents for maintaining a continuity between the new entity and the Divine. That is why we honor our fathers and mothers.

The creation of a child is a miracle made possible only by the force of life that comes from the Divine. In this process of conception, the essence of the Divine is transmitted through the birth parents to the child.

As for the behavior of the birth parents after conception, no matter how distasteful or disruptive, it cannot diminish or damage the life force breathed into the new being by the Divine. That life force flows directly to the new entity together with unique qualities and talents to be fully and freely expressed in harmony with other beings.

When we honor our fathers and mothers, we are acknowledging their irreplaceable function in the creation of our lives. We are also preparing our Selves to surrender to and align with the will of the Divine and the Divine's purpose for us that activates the creative expression of our talents.

Maintaining connection with the Divine is the single most significant factor in a person's life. However, that significance is no longer even considered by most of us. And, the Divine link from generation to generation, although present, is like an unread book, an unplugged microphone, an automobile without gasoline or a magnet wrapped in plastic.

The nature of a link is that it reaches in two directions. Those who choose to be that link, in this case a safe harbor for their children, must first re-establish connection with the Divine though their own birth parents. This is the only way the essence of the Divine can be transmitted to their children.

Being a safe harbor is a choice motivated by great intention and deep commitment. When that intention is present, the birth parents can begin activating their function of safe harbor by appreciating the three aspects of parenthood: the moment of conception, the link to the Divine and the gift of the creative process that is passed on to the child.

When a birth parent walks away from what he or she sets in motion in bringing a child into the world, the child feels that abandonment as real even though it exists only in the imagination of the parties. Instead of the comfort and loving guidance of a safe harbor, the child feels the hurt of being set adrift into a turbulent sea without a life preserver.

Although substitute parents cannot remove the hurt, they can, by being loving and supportive, prepare the way for an eventual reconnection with the birth parents. When the child makes that reconnection by honoring the father and mother as the vehicles through which his/her life came into being, the perceived abandonment or other unhappy experiences are recognized as the illusions they are. What is left is what has always been there: a whole and complete God Presence.

Life produces what appears to be an individual; but that appearance is an illusion disguising the truth that life is really a force encouraging everyone back to the Oneness.

We are each like a thread in a beautiful tapestry. Seeing and feeling the beauty and richness of everyone's contribution to that Divine work of art prepares us for our eventual and mandatory return to the Oneness together. We can then recognize the truth in the saying: "We are our brothers' keepers."

No children born in this realm can know that unless they honor their fathers and mothers: the essential vehicles for their existence. That is how true healing begins, a healing that only the Divine can provide, and that we encourage by surrendering our will to be separate and accept the truth that we are One.

This is the safest harbor of all: and, the only one available to beings born onto this realm.

CHAPTER 18

⌒

Meeting the Need

Remember, the desire for parents to fulfill their roles as loving, caring guides for their sons and daughters is always present. The desire of sons and daughters for that support is always present.

When you become aware that the desire is not being met, there is a solution. What you are experiencing in the physical is an outplaying of the beliefs you hold in consciousness. The seeming absence of the father or mother to the child, or the absence of the child to the parent is an illusion.

When the loving and caring guidance of either parent is not felt, bring that parent into your awareness and feel compassion for him or her. The apparent failings or absence were by agreement between you and the parent as part of your Phase One experience. Ask the Divine to heal the relationship, as you keep feeling the compassion.

Keep the Divine in your awareness and know that the healing that only the Divine can provide is occurring. Parents who are no longer living in this realm are not an exception. The force in the Universe's purpose to maintain your connection with them is always present.

Be patient and keep feeling the compassion that expands from your focus upon it. The healing occurs according to the Divine's timetable, not yours. Stay with the knowing that the healing continues as you continue feeling the compassion. The longer it takes, the more deeply you feel compassion not only for your parents, but also for everyone in your life.

If you are a father or mother who has freed a son or daughter under the mistaken assumption that they no longer need your loving and caring guidance, consider the following: Your daughter is expecting a man to be her safe harbor without the awareness that he cannot fulfill a role that only a father can provide; the man is suffering under the attempt to fulfill that role.

Feel deep compassion for both parties. They are doing the best they can. Bring them into your heart and keep them there as you ask the Divine to heal your relationships with them and their relationships with each other.

STRENGTHENING THE CONNECTION
TO YOUR SAFE HARBOR

The unconditional love and support of the Divine is always present in your life. Surrendering to that Divine Presence connects you with a safe harbor that underlies the one you are re-connecting to in the physical. Accepting the Divine as your safe harbor gives you the benefit of that immediate connection as well as the support to strengthen the connection to your human family.

The presence of the Divine as your safe harbor opens you to the compassion flowing through you from that Presence and inspires you to express compassion in all aspects of your life. Compassion is the basis of community from family to village to country to world.

Seeking Oneness and being connected to your safe harbor are essential prerequisites to satisfying and fulfilling relationships. Participation in and commitment to community is another prerequisite.

Two people joining together in the consciousness of independence from family and community are disavowing the Oneness. The absence of connection to family and community and expecting the other party to the relationship to meet that need set the stage for an unsatisfying relationship and increases the risk of failure.

Think of the Oneness (represented in the physical by family and community and supplemented by the Divine) as your safe harbor. We all need this and are seeking it even though awareness of that need is not present.

In the absence of connection to a safe harbor that includes the Divine, and a connection to community that includes the Oneness, we will not allow our Selves success in career and fulfilling relationships. Otherwise we are saying to our Selves we do not need the connections. However, our need to maintain these connections is too strong for us to override.

Surrendering to the Divine knowing that you are always unconditionally loved and supported and guided perfectly toward the Oneness frees you to move forward in all aspects of your life. Aligning your individual purpose (what you love to do) with Universal Purpose fills your purpose with Divine Power and what you love to do with the passion that prepares the way for achieving fulfillment in career and relationships.

What we are looking at is rebuilding families as the inner circles of communities that will provide the solid support for future generations. We start where we are.

Awaken in your consciousness the importance of genders and roles. Mothers and fathers play different roles in the family. The experience and wisdom of each provides the richness of family life. As a son or daughter, whatever your age, dig deep for the ways each parent really cared for and supported you. When you feel compassion for them over an extended period of time, you will uncover the caring and affection you hadn't previously recognized.

USING THE CURRENT SITUATION
TO YOUR ADVANTAGE

When you observe current society, there is a great imbalance in the way men treat women. If you are a male who does not love and appreciate women, you are seeing a reflection of the way you feel about your Self. Be aware that you are depriving your Self of satisfying and fulfilling relationships with women.

Remember, you created the existing situation, therefore you can un-create it. In order to feel more love and appreciation for your Self, feel compassion for your father. He is the one you created to model male behavior for you. Keep going deeper with the compassion you feel for him until you feel his unconditional love and appreciation for you, just the way you are.

Bring in the Divine to heal the relationship, and stand with the Divine on the side of the healing. Feel the unconditional love and support coming to you from the Divine guiding you to open to the flow of unconditional love and support from your parents.

Then, do the same with your mother. You are re-creating your family as the core of your safe harbor. Next, expand the safe harbor to other members of your family, followed by those in your local community. Keep going until you feel compassion for all in your world as you continue standing alongside the Divine as the healing progresses.

Stay aware that each person is a reflection of how you view and feel about your Self. Notice how your appreciation for your Self expands as your feeling of compassion increases.

If you are a male who loves and appreciates women, join in consciousness with other men who feel as you do. When that number grows large enough you will see a shift in everyone's consciousness.

If you are a woman who does not love and appreciate men, you are seeing a reflection of the way you feel about your Self. Be aware that you are depriving your Self of satisfying and fulfilling relationships with men. You can follow the above procedure suggested for men.

If you are a woman who loves and appreciates men, join in consciousness with other women who feel as you do. You will be supporting the men who feel as you do and hastening the time when that number grows large enough to create a shift in everyone's consciousness.

Finally, as you witness, any place in the world, the pain and suffering that strife and conflict cause, feel compassion for those who are suffering, but stand with the Divine on the side of healing. Avoid empathizing with those who are suffering. What you focus on expands. So, focus on the healing, and not on the pain and suffering.

CHAPTER 19

The Hidden Force

There are many factors that underlie the continual failure of our society to provide economic opportunity and support for those who are ready and willing to participate in the system. Even in so-called "good times" many are not able to find positions that allow them to cover even modest living expenses. Matching talent with position that can bring satisfying and fulfilling employment is, for most people, not even a consideration in our economic system.

Take a closer look at the following paragraph from Chapter 18 in the section entitled, "Strengthening the Connection to Your Safe Harbor."

> **In the absence of connection to a safe harbor that includes the Divine, and a connection to community that includes the Oneness, we will not allow ourselves success in career and fulfilling relationships. Otherwise we are saying to our Selves we do not need the connections. However, our need to maintain these connections is too strong for us to override.**

This helps you become aware that you are confronted with an unrelenting and powerful force that mandates the economic results you keep witnessing and reliving. This powerful force exists in your consciousness as a resistance to the flow of unconditional love through you. You can reduce this resistance by feeling compassion for your parents as you reconnect to your safe harbor.

A QUIET AND PEACEFUL REORGANIZATION

Clarity is the first step in improving the quality of our lives. The second step is using the Universal Principles for guidance. Readers of this book are seeking both. Those who are ready to act will feel so inspired.

There is no limit to how joyful and fulfilling our lives become when we feel the healing presence of the Divine coupled with making Oneness our purpose and intention. We cannot do this alone, for each of us has an essential contribution to make to the community—expressing, with passion, his/her talent (individual purpose). The combination of these individual contributions expands the feeling of wholeness for each and draws us closer to the Oneness that binds us all.

As for finding the passion that is waiting to be released, remember:

1. Oneness is our common purpose. The Universe's purpose for you is to direct you to Oneness.

2. Align your individual purpose, what you love to do (your talent) with the Universe's purpose for you. This opens your purpose to the flow of Divine Power filling what you love to do with the passion that prepares the way for achieving fulfillment in career and relationships.

3. Reclaim and maintain your connection with family and the Divine as your safe harbor.

LIVING WITH PASSION

You are a God Presence created by the Divine to have your unique Presence make the Universe a richer and more beautiful place. Furthermore, you are loved and supported unconditionally by the Universe at all times and under all circumstances. This love and support flows to you for being who you are, just the way you are.

Whenever you do not feel this, know you are overriding what is always present with beliefs that you have created. These beliefs make it seem that you are not the recipient of the flow of Divine Power (love) through you. Keep opening these beliefs and surrender the energy that is freed into alignment with the Divine.

Joyfulness is the feeling quality of the unconditional love of God that is flowing through you continuously. Joyfulness comes from your choice to surrender to and then align with that unconditional love, the only true power that contains all possibilities.

You are aware that abundance is your natural state, and the way to expand that abundance is to appreciate what you already have. This includes appreciating your Self as a God Presence with the talent(s) the Divine has given you and wishes you to enjoy.

You reciprocate by fully and freely expressing the talent(s) (doing what you love). This is your purpose and when aligned with the Universe's Purpose for you—embracing Oneness—infuses what you love to do with a passion that only the Divine can inspire, and prepares the way for achieving fulfillment in career and relationships.

Filled with gratitude for all that you have, in a state of surrender to all possibilities (alignment with the Divine), and feeling the passion of doing what you love, you go forth and manifest all the beauty and richness there is to behold, even finding richness and beauty in places that previously appeared to be barren and unforgiving.

When you have reached the place described in the prior paragraph, you are ready for envisioning: seeing and feeling the most beautiful and wonderful context and environment for the Divine to manifest through you. (Caveat: Leave the details of the manifestation to the Divine.) Continue with the envisioning until it feels real. That is how you prepare for the manifestation.

SUMMARY

When you give, know that you are creating a vacuum for more love and abundance to come in. Holding on to what you have is telling your Self you do not have enough. This sets in motion experiences of lack. What you focus on expands.

The game of life originates in consciousness and remains there. The physical has no power. The function of the physical is to remind you what beliefs you are holding in consciousness.

The abundance that shows up in the physical originates in your consciousness. The more expanded your consciousness (the fewer beliefs you hold in consciousness), and the deeper your gratitude for your Self as a Divine Being, the more open you are to the natural flow of abundance that you eagerly move out so that more can come in.

In a consciousness of abundance, what previously seemed like lack and limitation re-appears in the physical as a reflection of the abundance you have uncovered. The amount of love and joy, richness and beauty you can give and receive is unlimited.

Life is a communal experience. We are in it together, bound by the Oneness that we are forever seeking.

Focus on expanding your consciousness. Remember that the function of the physical is informational: reflecting to you the limitations you are still holding in your consciousness. Any attempts to improve events or circumstances in the physical are counterproductive. You are giving power and importance to the place where none exists; you are also reinforcing and solidifying the limitations in consciousness that demand the results you are judging.

Giving any importance or power to the physical, an illusion that exists only in your consciousness, keeps you in limitation. That is why you created this Phase One experience.

Expanding your consciousness gives you access to the higher and lighter energies. This is where you feel the freedom to express your talents in new and unique ways that, in turn, inspire others to express theirs.

Step back and allow the Universe (the Divine) to handle the details. The Divine, aware of all possibilities, brings you, as a gift, the most supportive and perfect events and circumstances. Sometimes what is most supportive is the reflection of a belief that is limiting more expansive possibilities. Your role is to feel the discomfort and call it what it really is: the joy that you have so carefully and diligently disguised by the belief. Stay aware of the results that keep showing up, and continue opening the energy in the beliefs that are producing the limitations and discomfort you are experiencing. Each time you release a belief you will expand your natural state of joyfulness.

Remember, when you step out and act as a creator, you are making believe that you have the power to improve the quality of your life. All real Power rests with the Divine. The power that you are making believe is real, creates only illusions. Since nothing you create is real, pain, lack and loss are illusions.

Start seeing and feeling your Self and those you are interacting with as children playing in a sandbox. You are using your imagination solely for your entertainment. This is a wonderful way to bring more joy into your life. Making believe you have the power to create other than an illusion that exists anywhere but in your imagination, assures that you become the victim of your creations. (See section entitled, Trust in the Abundance in Chapter 11)

When you are ready to accept that the Divine has the real Power, you will awaken to the truth that the Divine is always on your side, your best friend, filling your life with abundance and moving you toward the Oneness. This awakening encourages you to deepen your gratitude for this truth and surrender manifestation to the Divine.

Be aware that every belief you hold in consciousness was put there by you as the creator. Until a belief is released, you will see it play out in the physical. The time during which you are releasing beliefs while other beliefs are still in force requires patience and a very strong intention to continue. Remember, you cannot do this alone. Your life is a communal experience. When you have the intention, you will create the perfect people to join with and the perfect guidance to lead you.

Oneness is your natural state. Your creation of and devotion to separation is waiting to be released so that you can enjoy the freedom of doing what you love, with passion, in your natural state of peace, harmony and abundance with all others, your perfect community.

CHAPTER 20

Abundance Revisited

You have read about many ways to again have abundance be your natural state. However, there is one of those ways that must be in place before your natural state of abundance becomes real for you: feel the truth that you already have it all. In the absence of that feeling, you can be certain that you have the belief that lack is real. That means you continue to create evidence that you do not have enough.

Our money-driven society is based on the consciousness of lack. Anyone who seeks to have more money must be coming from a consciousness of lack. No one who knows and feels he/she has it all desires more. Consider your perception of air. You know there is enough for your next breath. You don't spend time desiring more.

Here are some suggestions for achieving the feeling that you already have it all:

Set the intention and make the commitment to do whatever it takes to achieve the feeling that you already have it all.

Re-read the book and notice the ways you have not opened beliefs that reinforce your consciousness of lack. Consider as an example the following process: You read about the Principle, "If others are not appreciating you, it means you are not appreciating your Self." You then reflect on ways you can appreciate your Self more. Connecting with your safe harbor comes to mind. You feel compassion for your father until you feel his deep love and appreciation for you. Then, you do the same with your mother. You bring in the Divine to support you in creating the healing of these relationships, as well as to feel gratitude for the unconditional love and support that is always flowing to you from that Source.

There is another way to access the abundance that is already present: Feel gratitude to the Divine for all the abundance you already have. Know that God wishes you to have an abundant life and has given you the freedom to choose how to find that abundance by doing what you love with passion, and seeing and feeling everything from the highest vantage point.

You raise your vantage point by feeling gratitude for the Source of all that is. This means knowing you are safe and secure in the unconditional love and support of the Divine.

In the absence of feeling deep and full appreciation for all that you already have, you are saying to the Universe that there is no point in sending you more. As you increase your appreciation for what you already have, and that includes relationships as well as things, you realize how much you have that is worthy of appreciation. This is your segue to knowing you already have it all. Continue expanding your feeling of appreciation until you feel you already have it all. That is when you realize how abundant the Universe is and how abundant your life is right here, right now.

As long as your intention and commitment remain in place, you will find the places to focus your attention. You will also create the perfect support to continue with the journey until you do know and feel that you have it all.

GIVING AND RECEIVING REVISITED

When you give something to someone, you are really giving to your Self. Having made the belief in separation seem real, you tend to overlook this truth. And, using your physical reality as confirmation, you overlook a way to have abundance be your natural state.

After accepting the truth that you are always giving to your Self, you are ready for the next truth: however you see and feel about the recipient is how you see and feel about your Self.

When you use money to express appreciation, how you feel about the recipient determines whether your expression of appreciation is real, and felt as such as you prepare to make the expression.

When you are ready, take a moment to feel much love and appreciation for the recipient. Then write the check, count the money and either hand or send the money maintaining the feeling of love and appreciation.

After you release the money, see and feel the recipient surrounded in great abundance, his or her life enriched by your gift. See and feel your expression of appreciation continue to expand as it moves out into the Universe enriching everyone.

As you go through your day, see and feel abundance moving through you and out into the Universe embracing everyone. See and feel the abundance coming back as you gratefully open wider and wider to receive. Do not hold onto money. Keep the flow going.

Holding on to money is telling your Self you are not already abundant, you do not already have it all. When you feel, in the present moment, that abundance is your natural state, abundance becomes your experience in the physical.

Returning to the Principle of Giving and Receiving, when the gift meets the foregoing criteria, the energy of love and appreciation and the abundance surrounding it, must return to you expanded. If that does not occur, something in your consciousness is limiting the flow back to and through you.

Remember, the only function of the physical is to give you information as to what is in your consciousness so that you can clear any beliefs that are bringing you a result opposite to your natural state. The belief has no power. You put the belief there. You can open the energy in the belief so the truth shines through.

Take some quiet time to feel what is really going on. With full intention to be aware of what is blocking the flow, the insight will come to you. Since doing this alone is close to impossible, ask for the guidance and support to open your Self to the free flow of love and abundance: your natural state. Be clear that the level of intention you have determines the result you achieve. The Universe is always on your side. Are you on your side?

COMMUNITY REVISITED

Fully aware that your life is a communal experience gives you the opportunity to consider ways to support community. One way stands out: the payment of taxes. The general resistance to what is a contribution to community begins with creations in Phase One to make separation our reality.

When you open to the awareness that seeking Oneness is your main purpose, you can expect that beliefs you hold that subvert that purpose will come to your attention. If you feel discomfort when you send money to the government, you are ready to open beliefs that are disguising the joy of giving to your Self.

Government is not a power outside of you. Government is a creation in your imagination that exists only in your consciousness. As your creation, you determine the quality of your relationship with that creation. Seen and felt as a reflection of the Oneness, giving generously enriches your experience of Oneness. Also, giving generously opens the space for more to come in.

GRATITUDE REVISITED

Feeling gratitude is the way you connect with the Divine, the way you thank God for all that is, including the capacity to feel gratitude. Feeling gratitude takes you beyond the physical in the search for God, in the search for the meaning of life. Feeling gratitude for the Divine acknowledges that your purpose and your intention is to journey back to the Oneness that is the Divine. Feeling gratitude enriches every experience you have by reminding you that within that experience is the love of God.

GRATITUDE AND APPRECIATION

Feeling appreciation connects you with the illusions you have created, grounds you in the physical, and opens you to your creations. In feeling appreciation, the source is you, giving you a sense of control over your creations.

Feeling gratitude opens you to the Divine and is a relinquishment of control. In feeling gratitude, both the Source and the recipient is the Divine.

COMPASSION

When we resonate with the pain and suffering someone is experiencing, we express compassion by offering support that brings some degree of comfort to the sufferer. This is the first step. Next, comes the support in consciousness. This is opening your heart as you feel compassion (a combination of unconditional love and appreciation) for the person(s) silently saying, for example, "I love and appreciate you for volunteering to reflect the illusion of pain and suffering that I created as real in my consciousness. I am praying to the Divine to support me in seeing and feeling you as who you really are—the Power and Presence of God—so that I see and feel my Self the same way. As this truth becomes real for me, you no longer need to reflect the illusion. And, we both enjoy doing what we love in mutual support: the success of each celebrated as the success of both. I feel gratitude to God for the gift of compassion, and the healing that is already taking place."

CHAPTER 21

⤙⤚

The Circle of Love and Joyfulness

The Circle of Love and Joyfulness is a community intentionally created by those who have chosen to use Universal Principles and the concepts that align with them as the guidelines for interaction with one another. This book describes these guidelines as they have expanded as a result of that interaction.

A natural outgrowth of playing together in this way has been a steady expansion of consciousness that has freed creative expression—doing what we love for the joy of the experience. This has led to a new way of being in business.

Business as defined by Circle Members is two or more people with complementary profiles committing to each other to joyfully do what they love as a process of consciousness expansion. This interaction creates a new and expanded energy that inspires creative expression, which transforms existing businesses or the creation of a new one into a joyful and fulfilling game.

The spiritual practice of the participants includes continually surrendering to the All, feeling gratitude for receiving from the All, and giving from having it all, so that more flows through.

We know that joyfully doing what we love is an expression of appreciation for our Selves and for the Universe that has gifted us the talents that we love to express. Joining with others who are doing what they love, with passion, as described in Chapter 19 in the section entitled, "A Quiet and Peaceful Reorganization" brings us a level of joyfulness and fulfillment far beyond what we thought possible.

Playing together in business in this new way has inspired the creation of a handbook for Circle Members entitled, "Go Into Business with Confidence." The handbook describes the elements common to all businesses as well as the state of consciousness that leads to a satisfying, fulfilling and joyful experience for all.

Since the Circle of Love and Joyfulness contains participants with a broad range of talents and personality profiles, it has become a resource to support participants as they explore whole new ways of playing together, and with others, in business.

A primary focus of the Circle is raising the level of joyfulness of the participants. This is the most direct way to expand consciousness and create events and circumstances that must reflect the expanding joyfulness. That is also what I love to do.

CHAPTER 22

Frequently Asked Questions

ONENESS AND SEPARATION

Question:

I am confused. You say that there isn't anybody except our self, that we make up everyone else, and that I am only talking to myself. Then later you say not to go from phase one to phase two alone, that I am supposed to do it with support. Help me with this.

Answer:

You are the Power and Presence of God making believe you are a mere human. Your Divine Self includes all Selves. However, you came into the Human to experience the opposite—seeming separation from those you interact with.

Everything you experience is in your consciousness. Those you interact with are aspects of your Self. They reflect how you see and feel about your Self.

There is a companion concept: you see and feel the events and circumstances of your day at your present level of consciousness. Your consciousness is limited by the beliefs you hold. Every belief limits your experience of your natural state. As you open the energy in a belief you move closer to your natural state. As you continue with that process, everything you experience becomes richer and fuller; people whom you previously thought had little to offer become sources of inspiration and expanded creative expression. You see ways to interact with those whose talents (what they love to do) perfectly complement your own.

When you have a real intention to create that expansion, you attract the perfect support to guide you through the expansion.

VALUING

Question:

I find my Self short of money all of the time. I practice frugality, and am very careful what I spend my money on. Do you have any suggestions?

Answer:

We determine the value of everything in our lives. In our money-oriented society, we demonstrate our value assessments by what we pay for, and how much we pay. Many of us have been trained to believe that the less we spend for something the better. Therefore, we often unwittingly place little or no value on things that have great value: teachers who inspire their students, and social workers and nurses who are loving and caring to their clients and patients.

Since we are also trained to believe that our abundance is limited, we diminish our valuations to conform to our perception of diminished capacity to pay. The solution lies in the companion of valuing—appreciation.

Appreciation is the feeling quality that gives value its power and opens the door to our abundance. We are feeling beings and we connect with our power through our feelings. When we allow our Selves to deeply appreciate what we value, we are in closer touch with the abundance that is all around us. Knowing and feeling that we have it all allows the abundance into our lives.

Feeling appreciation is the first part of a two-step process. The second part is expressing the appreciation, and since money is involved, the expression is with money. This is how you take the power out of money and free money to do what it loves, express appreciation.

You can feel as much appreciation as you wish since the flow of appreciation through you is unlimited. Money, as an expression of appreciation is also unlimited.

Thus, we complete the circle. Having decided that something is of great value, we feel and then express appreciation to demonstrate our appreciation for the value we are receiving.

The capacity to feel appreciation is an extraordinary gift that the Universe has bestowed upon us as we relate to our physical world. To take full advantage of this gift, I suggest the following sequence: Feel gratitude to the Divine, the Source of your capacity to feel appreciation. The flow of energy you feel from your connection to and gratitude for this Presence activates your capacity to feel appreciation for your Self. This places you in the perfect position to appreciate everything, and reinforces in your consciousness your Oneness with all that is.

The more you practice feeling gratitude to the Divine, the more reasons you find to feel appreciation for all the abundance in your physical world. What is better than a life full of people and things that you value and appreciate? What is better than knowing you have it all so that you freely and joyfully express appreciation? Practicing feeling and expressing appreciation is a gift that expands infinitely in all directions. Have fun! (see Chapter 20 "Abundance Revisited")

EXPANDING OUR VISION

Question:

I have a friend in her early 20s who is suffering from many health problems, and I'm trying to figure out how I can support her?

Answer:

The best way to support her is to see her whole and complete as the God Presence that she really is. She is not her physical body. In order to do this, you first have to see your Self the same way.

As you seek to support your friend, recognize that she is giving you a wonderful gift. Take advantage of this gift, and show your appreciation for the gift by seeing the truth behind the veil of physicality.

Seeing our physicality as though we are simply physical beings is like a dog chasing its tail. When we see our physicality from the vantage point of the God Presence, we appreciate that the physical experiences we have created are just a purposeful excursion into Self-imposed limitations. When we are ready to expand our vision, the Universe provides us with the perfect support to open to the power we have hidden in our beliefs in limitation.

Expanding our vision means opening ourselves to being the God Presence. Take some time to visualize or feel your Self as more than just a physical presence. When you are in that expanded energy, embrace your Self as a physical being and feel appreciation for the experiences you have had and continue to have as such an entity. Appreciate all the courage it has taken for you to create a life of perceived powerlessness and limitation. Feel appreciation for all those people who have supported you in having those experiences.

See the continuity in the progression from first creating and then seeing and feeling life from the vantage point of a physical being to one as the God Presence.

As for the healing of the health problems, only the Divine heals. Your role is to feel compassion for your friend as you invite the Divine in to bring about the healing.

Do not focus on the health problems. What you focus on expands. Focus on staying on the side of the Divine, continuing to feel compassion.

COMPETITION

Question:

My five-year-old son has recently gotten into BMX racing. I'm uncomfortable with the competitiveness of it. Am I going against principle by letting him do it or has he chosen it him Self as an experience/learning tool and it is not about what I think at all?

Answer:

The responses we have to any event or circumstance tells us what we believe about our Selves, and the world around us. Your son's choice of a competitive activity has aroused both doubt and trust in the wisdom of his choice. This tells you about your view of competition.

Competition is neither good nor bad. It is a form of interaction that you may relate to in many different ways. Instead of looking at it in the traditional way, you may see it as an opportunity to express the best that is in you, rather than as a way to be better than another participant.

In fact, you may see the situation as a mutually-supportive activity where all participants are really on the same side rather than on opposite sides. If this approach feels good to you, your son will easily pick up on your new view of his activity.

You and your son are in parallel and interwoven universes at the same time. He reflects your state of consciousness: everything you do, say or feel.

This is perfect support for you. The more appreciation you feel for him, the more appreciation he will feel for you as well as for him Self. The more appreciation you feel for him, the more appreciation you will feel for your Self.

There is so much love to be shared here. Enjoy!

JUDGMENT

Question:

The recurring difficulty I experience while working at releasing judgment is my inability to view things like murder, rape, violence, etc. as just events neither right nor wrong. Using the example of Hitler and the Nazis for instance, how would you suggest I deal with this?

Reply:

Every experience we have is created in our imagination. The experience is not real, just made to seem real.

Each of us is free to see life any way we wish. If we choose to accept the belief in "right" and "wrong," whatever we judge becomes for us the way we judge it. If I insist on seeing some people as "bad" and call them "criminals," I create those kinds of people in my experiences. They will continue to behave in ways that justify my judgment of them.

Our criminal justice system is a perfect example. We judge people we call criminals as "bad" and they keep acting in ways that support our view of them. As a society, this judgment has led us in ever-expanding circles for many years.

As soon as anyone is willing to release a judgment of someone, the energy that is frozen in place by the judgment is freed. All energy is love and we are free to use it in any way that we wish. We can use the energy to support our belief in "right" and "wrong," or we can free it to embrace, nurture and harmonize all it touches.

Each of us is the whole of the Universe and all that we see is our Selves. Horror and misfortune are in the eye of the beholder. So are beauty, wonder and magnificence. We are each free to choose what to see in each moment.

In order to see beauty, wonder and magnificence, we first rise to a higher place by releasing beliefs that limit our view of the event or circumstance. When you set the intention to see things from a higher perspective, the perfect support appears to guide you to that expanded consciousness.

CORE BELIEFS

Question:

My core belief = I'm bad. I felt separated from my parents, since I felt they did not understand me, they didn't understand where I was coming from, and because they were not even interested in how I felt. They seemed only interested in me obeying their every command and to be willing to do things that I didn't enjoy or things I hated, without any talking back. My mother's famous words were "As long as you live under this roof, you will do as I say!" Since my structural belief is that "I'm bad" or Selfish, I have difficulty in loving that belief or appreciating it. I think this has been my main problem—I dislike having the "I'm bad" belief so much and I want to look good so much (so others don't see the real me as "bad" as I subconsciously think) that I am willing (reluctantly) to do things I dislike.

Answer:

Thank you for your honesty and your clarity.

First of all, be aware that many people have a core belief similar to yours. Next, remember that you went to great lengths to acquire and experience the core belief, and your parents went to great lengths to support you in acquiring and experiencing the belief. Finally, remember that every experience you have is created in your imagination—not real, just made by you to seem real.

You are all on the same side even though you perceive that you are on opposite sides. Taking your parents out of their adversarial role and into a supportive role will go a long way toward opening your energy around this core issue.

As for the core belief, there are really two parts to it. The first is the belief that you are "bad." The second is the belief that you have to be accommodating to people so that they will like you in spite of the fact that you are "bad."

As for opening the energy bound in the belief that you are "bad," the first step is to acknowledge the part of you that has created the belief. Appreciate how clever and resourceful this part of you has been to sell you this untruth.

The second step is to allow your Self to feel all the energy in the belief free of the label "bad." When you are able to feel all that energy, open your heart and feel love for it. This energy is the Power of God flowing through you. As you do these steps over and over again, you will feel your Self regaining a sense of the Divine Being you really are.

Remain conscious of your need to please others. Notice how this need weakens as you open the energy around the belief that you are "bad."

Be patient and kind to your Self.

Finally, re-read Chapter 17 for guidance in satisfying the desire in you to have a safe harbor and the desire in your parents to provide it for you.

Comment from Questioner:

I sat in on a mutual support group meeting as you suggested. I found the meeting to be very uplifting and supportive. I enjoyed it a lot. What I sense is that if I had a woman in my life that was like those in the mutual support group and also was associated with co-workers of the same supportive nature, it would not matter much at all that I still had the belief that I was bad or Selfish. Because even if I wasn't giving fully, the other person whom I would be relating to would still be supportive and understanding and loving in word and deed, in general. There wouldn't be much need for me to handle the undesired internal belief.

Response:

What you have stated is again a very common belief. Holding onto this belief is a perfect way to avoid opening the energy that is making you so uncomfortable.

The people in your life, particularly your parents, are the perfect people to be there. You are all in support of each other. You didn't make any mistake nor did they. No one wandered into each other's life by accident.

If you were to move or change your employment you would remain in the same feeling state. The new people in your life would look and feel just like the ones you left.

There is one constant in your life and that is you. As long as you hold onto a belief, you will keep experiencing the out-playing of that belief. Those you interact with have to reflect it to you as long as it remains in your consciousness.

You came here to feel love for your Self and all of the other people in your life just the way you all are. You also came here to appreciate them for their remarkable support of you, and to appreciate your Self for your willingness to go into these uncomfortable feelings.

There is no way to finesse or do an end run around opening your beliefs and re-connecting with your safe harbor. Your awareness has increased immeasurably and will continue to increase as you proceed. And as much as possible, lighten up; remind your Self, this is all in your imagination.

ANGER

Question:

When I get angry is it really someone else's anger? Someone else is viewing my anger and it's not really mine, it's theirs?

Answer:

You cannot resonate with a feeling unless you have that feeling. If it appears that you are witnessing someone else's anger, and you are able to feel any of it, the anger is a reflection of your anger.

You are the whole of the Universe and all that you see is your Self. Turning this around so that you become the mirror rather than the one looking in the mirror is just a way to avoid both accepting how powerful a creator you are, and the support you are being offered.

There is no Power in the mirror. You have hidden that Power in your beliefs. The extraordinary gift you are being offered is the opportunity to see everything as a reflection of those beliefs. When you open the Power in the beliefs, It will flow through you as love—the only energy in the Universe. We give this energy many names including "anger" to give us different kinds of human experiences.

Whenever you notice you are calling an energy something other than love, see if you can remove the label you have assigned to the energy and feel the love. The more willing you are to acknowledge that all energy is love, the more joy you will allow into your life.

Question:

When you talk about "opening up the energy around your anger," do you mean that all the experiences that we have in our lives are really just opportunities to experience all sorts of emotions and then move on? For instance, if you get angry over something, do you mean that you should just feel the feeling of anger and that the incident which caused the emotion is irrelevant—just a means to an end? If so, is it pointless to plan your life in order to avoid incidents where negative emotions could be created, e.g., avoiding someone whom you know you always end up in an argument with?

Answer:

When your heart is open wide, the love of the Divine flows freely through you and you feel joyful. When you wish to experience something other than joyfulness, you close your heart restricting the flow of energy. One way you do this is by judging someone's actions as unacceptable.

When you are ready to open the energy you have labeled "anger", broaden your view of the situation. This means acknowledging that you have chosen to create the judgment, and that those participating with you are volunteering their support. When you open your heart in appreciation for their loving support, you free up the flow of Divine Power through you.

FORGIVING YOUR SELF

Question:

I am trying to find a way to forgive my Self for something I feel is really horrible. I am a 51 year-old man who about 20 years ago left my wife and kids. At the time I felt it was the best thing to do. I felt overwhelmed with responsibility, angry to an extreme and was physically abusive to my kids. The only contact I have had with them has been in sending them money over the years. After reading your books it sounds like you are saying that the principle of perfection would say that what I did was OK but I can't seem to accept that. I have had these horrible feelings for 20 years and I would like to unload this burden and see how my kids turned out. Do you have any advice?

Answer:

Your focus is absolutely correct. This is about you forgiving your Self. Your belief about your behavior (terrible), and your label for your feelings (horrible) provided you with hiding places for the love that allowed you to have the familial experiences you have had.

Before you came into the human, you intended to create these experiences. Your family members agreed to play the supportive roles. You are all in this together in mutual support.

You have started the process of forgiving your Self. Being clear on the complicity of your family releases them from their roles as victims and frees you of the guilt that precludes your willingness to forgive your Self. The next step in the process is appreciating how courageously the participants in your situation have been performing their roles. This includes you.

There are no mistakes or accidents in the Universe. Everything that happens is purposeful. And, each participant is a volunteer in support of all the other participants.

Following the foregoing suggestions is simpler if you step back from the situation and view it from a broader perspective. Open your Self to see the situation and the participants as part of a Divine exploration—a courageous attempt to expand the Divine conscious-ness through the exploration of the human experience. See the par-ticipants as who they truly are: the God Presence.

No one can be hurt because you are not separate entities, and this is all taking place in your imagination. When you are able to enjoy who you really are, your joy is felt by all who join with you in what you call a human tragedy but is really a human celebration.

You believe that your behavior was "wrong." The belief in "right" and "wrong" is a choice we make to give our Selves the experiences that result from that belief.

Remember, we are all the God Presence. We are not who we make believe we are. We have had to create many contrivances to keep our Selves away from the truth of our real nature, which is to love un-conditionally. The main vehicle that we all use to give our Selves our human experiences is being judgmental.

As for visiting your children, after you feel forgiveness for your Self, you will sense the perfect time to visit with them.

Re-read Chapter 17 and satisfy your desire to reconnect with your safe harbor (parents and the Divine). This will prepare you to be the safe harbor for your family as you ready your Self to become a mutu-ally-supportive family.

DEATH—NO ONE REALLY DIES

From a Letter:

". . . It has been a very rough year . . . I lost my two very dear brothers and my lovely sister-in-law within a four month time. It was a very, very troubled time for me. As my husband said, since I love deeply, I hurt deeply . . . It is especially hard to see their young children grow up without them . . .

. . . The support from my community when my family members passed was tremendous . . . Truly all is well in my world and I have a great life and much to be grateful for . . ."

Reply:

The difficulty you are having in accepting the circumstances you describe is understandable. However, there are no accidents or mistakes in the Universe, and you obviously chose to open the energy around what you call "death." In order for the events to appear real, you need others to play the roles that you describe.

No one really dies. Those of us who choose to experience human form give up memory of who we really are, but only temporarily.

As we open the energy in beliefs in how limited and powerless we are, we become aware of how unlimited and powerful we really are. Eventually, we confirm with eyes that see beyond our own dimension that there is no "death," and that those who shared time with us as humans are continuing on their journey just as we are.

Since we are all One, each journey enriches everyone. You have much to be thankful for, as you note in your letter, and your capacity to uncover the joy in all of life is truly unlimited.

You may wish to communicate with those family members who have moved on. My way of connecting is to open my heart and feel deep unconditional love for them, as I feel their deep unconditional love for me. I know they wish the best for me, and I can feel that support. The time I spend in this way is very inspiring and energizing.

Everyone's experiences in life are unique. Trust your Self to give and receive unconditional love without limitations of any kind. And enjoy what happens.

CHAPTER 23

~

Universal Principles

(REVISED FOR THIS EDITION OF *The Journey*)

Universal Principles are the guidelines that govern our lives perfectly.

1. Energy

The basic component of the Universe, energy, occurs in either materialized or un-materialized form. All that we see and feel is an expression of energy.

All energy is the love of the Divine flowing through us. When we resist the flow of love, we experience discomfort. When we align with the love, we feel joyful and at peace.

2. Infinite Intelligence, or God

Within all energy is an intelligence that is infinite, eternal and purposeful. This Infinite Intelligence, which we sometimes refer to as God, or simply love, is the source of all creative expression and the essential Power in the Universe.

The way we view our Infinite Intelligence, or God, is precisely the way we see and feel about our Self and the way we experience life. When we perceive God as an unconditionally loving and supportive energy at all times and under all circumstances, we experience our world as totally safe, and everyone in it as loving and supportive.

3. Oneness

Since the essence of everything is pure loving energy, in the truest sense, *we are One*. Oneness, love, is indivisible. Whenever we attempt to withhold love from anyone, we withhold love from everyone, including our Self. The truth of this Principle becomes clear as we allow our hearts to open and feel our interconnectedness.

4. There Is Nothing Outside Of Us

In order to have our human experiences, we have created the apparent reality that we are living outside the Oneness; that there are things and people that can affect us without our consent. The truth is that there is nothing outside of us; all that we see is our Self. This becomes our new reality when we open the belief in separation and accept the truth that we are One.

5. Perfection

God is perfect and expresses this perfection as unconditional love and support. Whatever unfolds is God happening. When we see and feel other than unconditional love, we are seeing and feeling the disguises we have created with our beliefs. We create disguises to explore the experiences that make up our human journey.

When we are ready to see and feel with greater clarity, we embrace whatever is before us in unconditional love, trusting that the Universe, in Its constant expression of unconditional love, is sending us the perfect support to expand our joyfulness. With practice, our clarity grows, along with our gratitude for the unconditional love, support and joyfulness that is always present.

6. Beliefs

A belief is a thought hooked to a feeling. The feeling gives the thought a perception of power and creates an illusion that is experienced as real. Under the guidance of our Souls, we adopt beliefs to provide us with the precise experiences we are having, and that we planned before we entered this realm. The urge to explore life beyond our beliefs is a signal that our Soul Selves are ready to guide us in freeing the flow of Divine Love, disguised by our beliefs.

7. Feelings

Our Soul communicates to us through our feelings. The more willing we are to feel our feelings, the more able we are to connect with the love that resides in them.

Love, fully, freely and joyfully felt is the true Power in the Universe—a totally peaceful Power. This Power does not belong to each of us; It emanates from the Divine and manifests through us when we surrender to It.

8. Mutual Support

Our Universe functions as a mutual support system in which each and every thing in existence relates to and affects every other thing. Every person and circumstance in our lives is there to support us by reflecting back to us the beliefs we hold in our consciousness.

The prevalent belief that we are naturally competitive and adversarial is just a mirroring back to us of our acceptance of that belief. Releasing beliefs from our consciousness frees the love of God to flow through us and to those with whom we interact. Mutual support then reflects more of our natural state of Oneness, and becomes the foundation for rebuilding community based on love, from family to village, city, state, nation and world. The more we look for the love that is present in each event and circumstance in our lives, the more we appreciate how perfect the Universe's support for us truly is.

9. The Mirror Principle

Everything we see and feel is a reflection of the state of our own consciousness. Every person we attract into our lives is showing us a perception we hold about our Selves. Every feeling expressed by another mirrors a feeling deep within us. This reflection is a gift, for it allows us to be aware of the beliefs we hold, and the ways we have blocked the free flow of Divine Love through us.

10. Non-judgment

At our request, we have been carefully taught to evaluate and judge much of what we experience. However, "right" and "wrong," "good" and "bad" are just beliefs, disguises for the unconditional love that is always present.

The truth is that everything that occurs is just another event or circumstance that we have created in our imagination. Judging something keeps whatever we judge the way we judge it. Also, judging anyone or anything tells us that we are judging our Selves in the same way.

Judging creates discomfort that can only be relieved by opening our hearts, first to the judgment and then to the person or thing we have judged. Freeing this open-hearted energy leads to the joyful feeling of unconditional love for our Selves as the wholeness and completeness of who we really are.

11. Purpose

The Universe's purpose for each of us is to direct us to Oneness. When we align our individual purpose, what we love to do (our talent), with the Universe's purpose, the flow of Divine Power fills what we love to do with passion. This prepares the way for achieving fulfillment in career and relationships.

12. Comfort and Discomfort

Our bodies are magnificent instruments that we create to support us in having the experiences we come to the human to have. Our bodies are created and maintained in consciousness. They mirror the state of our consciousness, beliefs in how to look, act, age and die.

Unencumbered by beliefs, our consciousness is unlimited. The natural state of our consciousness is perfect ease, as is the natural state of our bodies. The beliefs we have about our bodies are there to love and embrace just the way they are. The resulting expansion of consciousness shifts the bodies' state from that of un-ease to ease.

13. *Abundance*

Abundance is our natural state. Everything we experience is an aspect of the abundance. When limitation appears, we are seeing a reflection of our beliefs, a resistance we have created to knowing we have it all. Opening these beliefs provides us with a clearer view of the abundance that is all around us awaiting our feeling of gratitude. Feeling gratitude for what we presently have opens us to knowing we have it all.

14. *Giving and Receiving*

Giving and receiving always occur in balance. It is natural to receive gratefully and to give generously: an expression of appreciation for the gift we have received. The corollary to the Principle of Giving and Receiving is that we give only to our Selves knowing we already have it all.

15. *Non-attachment and Freedom*

Our perceived need to hold on to anything or anyone demonstrates our belief in shortage and personal incompleteness. Holding on to anything—people or possessions —blocks the flow of love through us thereby reducing the joy of our experience with the person or object. Holding onto what we have also inhibits new people and new things, along with the new experiences they bring, from coming into our lives.

As we open our hearts, feel our state of Oneness and expand our trust in the natural abundance of the Universe, we give our Selves and everyone else the gift of freedom.

16. *Means and Ends*

Means and ends are the same. The action and outcome are one. To achieve peace, we feel and express inner peacefulness. To enjoy a life that works perfectly, we see and feel the perfection of everything and everyone, including our Selves. To experience the natural abundance of the Universe, we feel and express gratitude for the abundance we already have.

17. Harmony in Relationships

Our primary relationship is with God. How we see and feel about God determines the quality of all our relationships. Knowing that God loves and supports us unconditionally, allows each of us to feel unconditional love and support for our Selves. We are then able to feel and express unconditional love and support for everyone.

Aligning with this sequence allows you to see your Self and others as who you really are: the Power and Presence of God eager to surrender to all possibility. When you hold this Truth in your consciousness that is what is reflected to you.

18. The Universe Handles the Details

The Universe handles the details of our lives in accordance with the beliefs we hold in consciousness. Our core belief is to supersede the Divine in how we live our lives. The sole purpose of that belief and all the others we have created is to give us a life opposite to our natural state.

As we open the energy in our beliefs, we increase the flow of Divine Love into all aspects of our lives. We can then rest in the arms of the Divine and observe the details of our day reflect the joy that the Love releases.

19. What You Focus on Expands

The flow of Divine Power (Love) through the beliefs you hold in consciousness manifest as limitations in your physical reality. Focus on the physical brings you more of the limitations your existing beliefs are creating. Focus on releasing beliefs and surrendering to all possibility frees the flow of Divine Power to manifest more richness, beauty and joy in your life.

CHAPTER 24

❧

Meditations from Grady Claire Porter

THIS IS THE WAY I START MY DAY

I absolutely adore who I am!

I am totally enchanted with every aspect of my life!

I fully appreciate the richness and support each event of my day brings!

And, I consistently allow my Self to feel the Love the Universe showers upon me, and all else, in this beautiful, infinite day!

MORNING FOCUS

I awaken in total trust that everything the Universe brings me in this day is a gift of love and support. I feel deep appreciation for these gifts and I unconditionally accept them all. I see the activities of my day as an experience and expression of my expanded Soul awareness, and I rejoice in all of them, exactly as they are. I feel the abundance

Grady Claire Porter is a spiritual coach and the author of *Conversations with JC,* volumes 1, 2 and III.

115

bestowed upon me by the Universe, and I joyfully accept all the riches inherent in this day. I am committed to an ever-expanding awareness of who I really am. I am in absolute trust that I am unconditionally loved and supported by the Universe and all in it; and I, in accepting that love and support, express it fully to all I see and interact with.

EVENING FOCUS

How grateful I am for all the gifts of this day. Thank you Universe for loving and supporting me so gently and wisely. I feel deep appreciation for my willingness to accept your gifts and I feel blessed by each of them. I rejoice in my expanding awareness of my Soul Self, and in the love and support I receive for this expansion. I rest confidently and comfortably knowing that my human Self is now renewed to play some more.

BE-ATTITUDES

1. I am in the high joy vibration.
2. I am fulfilling my purpose in expanding my view of the Divine.
3. I am releasing any perception that would cloud my view of the Divine in all things.
4. I am releasing any judgment of my Self, of anyone else, or any condition. Whatever is, is perfect.
5. I am releasing any fear, any doubt, any anger, any illusion that I perceive would separate me from the infinite love of the Divine.
6. I am aware of, accepting and acknowledging the perfection of each moment in my experience.
7. I am aware of, accepting and acknowledging that I chose this human experience to remember and practice my perfection.

8. I am in absolute trust that I am constantly and consistently in alignment with Principle, God.

9. I am be-ing on purpose. There is nothing for me to do to be on purpose.

10. I am expressing unconditional love in everything I do.

11. I am choosing peace and joy in all situations and under every circumstance.

12. I am open and willing to allow the Divine to express in me, through me, as me.

APPRECIATION

Appreciation is the ever-expanding energy of valuing. Appreciation is the joyful expression of acceptance of one's Self as the all in all. In the human, the act of true appreciation is the greatest gift we give ourselves. Affording others the opportunity to appreciate extends and expands this gift.

You are focused on appreciation. You give yourself the opportunity to BE appreciation; to BE the ever-expanding energy of valuing your Self and all you create.

You have two words you use often: "Thank You". You give yourself the opportunity now to expand on that expression. First, feel the appreciation for whatever event (and all those in the event) that you create. Feel appreciation for yourself for the creation. Be clear that "Thank You" "I appreciate You" is a conversation with your Self. All those you create in your experience are there to reflect that appreciation back to you.

I have said to you "money's only purpose is to express appreciation" and that is so. That is not a limiting concept of money. Indeed, it is the most expansive energy that we can express and money is delighted to be the tangible expression of that energy.

The opportunity that you have now is to be clear about the vast amount of your Soul power you disguised as money. In setting up a limited economic structure where money had all the power to provide happiness and well-being, stature and acclaim (or to take it away) you were able to play the game of limitation and struggle. And now, as you embark on this new game of unconditional appreciation for yourself and that Self that you hid away, you can truly marvel at the unlimited creative being you are and free money up to do what it loves to do: EXPRESS APPRECIATION!

As money flows in and out of your experience in joyful appreciation, be clear that it is not the source of your abundance nor is it a measure of it. Be clear that abundance is the infinite, unbounded richness of all we are. Abundance is the essence of our ever-expanding experience and expression of appreciation. Money is just one of the infinite number of ways in the human that we create to express appreciation. I appreciate you.

YOU ARE LIKE A CREEK BED

(In response to a request for guidance whether we should pursue moving the office, moving to a bigger house, taking a trip to Russia, etc., He said to me:)

What difference does it make? Concern yourself with the activity of God within you. Do not bother with trying to set up the outer activities. Express unconditional love and peace in everything you do.

It doesn't matter what you do, if you are expressing God. You are like a creek bed. Your sole purpose is to provide the place for the flow, through you. If just one drinks from your water, you have served your purpose. Do you think the creek bed envies the pond where many drink? And, does the creek bed worry where it's going next? No, it knows the flow through it will determine its shape, form and direction.

Creek beds are nourished and fed by the flow of good through them. That's not the purpose of the flow, but a natural consequence of it. If you, as a creek bed, should grow something inside you that would dam up or block the flow, all you have to do is release, and the flow will take it away.

Creek beds don't worry or fret. They just are. They are wide open so the flow can move through them joyously and uninterruptedly; they are available so that the loving flow within them can be partaken of effortlessly; they are gentle and flexible so that, should the flow need to move to other areas to nourish, it can widen or push its banks at will; they are constantly refreshed by the newness of the pure, fresh, sparkling flow infinitely moving through them.

THE HIGH JOY VIBRATION

What is the high joy vibration? A world of unconditional love and abundance. A world peopled by those doing what they really love to do for the sheer and absolute joy of being what they really love to be, sharing for the sheer joy of sharing. A world wherein each idea supports all other ideas. A world of oneness, each participant 100% committed to adding his or her infinite individuality to the whole. A world of perfection infinitely expressing and experiencing itself. A world of absolute trust in each other and in the perfection that we all are. A world of absolute beauty, infinite life, harmony, peace. A world of purpose, wherein each concordantly and exquisitely fits with the other.

This is not a "dream world." It is a world without dreams -- perceptions. It is the real world that you can experience here and now: a world you can live in, love in, enjoy, share. And you have the key to this world. Release the belief in the power of money, and accept the infinite availability and supply of abundance. There is no limit, no boundaries, no end to this world. Accept it. Acknowledge it. Experience it—now!

THE PEACE EXERCISE

The Peace Exercise is not just an activity. It is a way of life for you from this point on. It is a way to feel the love you have for each part of your Self that you have not yet been ready to unconditionally accept. It is the red carpet for this planet to move forward into absolute joy and harmony. For I tell you this, as you totally and unconditionally love your Self, at all times and under all circumstances, you are the High Joy Vibration. And the power of that enlightens the consciousness of whomever and wherever your love and thought are focused.

There are two things that will alert you to begin the Peace Exercise. First, at any time you feel you wish to change *anything or anyone*, you are giving your Self the opportunity to experience the power of peace. The second is justification. At any time you feel you must justify anything, to your Self or anyone else, you are telling your Self you are ready to practice the power of peace.

Now be clear on this. Change and justification are not bad. The desire to change and justify is not bad. Both simply come into your experience to support you in doing what you love to do—*being the power of peace.*

Peace Exercise

I feel, with unconditional trust, that I am the whole of the Universe, and all that is seen and unseen is Me.

I feel, at my deepest level, the power of being who I am.

I feel the willingness and the readiness to exercise the power of being who I am.

I feel the gentleness of my own power, and the absolute certainty of knowing that my power is the power of peace.

I feel the conviction and trust of my Self so totally that I no longer need to project anything but absolute and unconditional love.

I feel, in totality, the infinite variety of my beingness.

I feel the warmth and peace of unconditionally loving my own infinite Self.

And, at this deep feeling level, I this moment yield to the power of my Self, totally trusting my unconditional love and support for all of Me, and accept all that I see as the expression and experience of this power.

EXALTATION

Since in your language "Invocation" is a plea or prayer for support; and since we are playing at a much higher game of acknowledging, accepting and appreciating everything as omniscient support; and since you are committed to ever expanding your experience and expression of perfection; I give you "Exaltation," a highly intensified sense of well-being and power.

I am in total harmony with the perfection of the Universe.

I absolutely trust that this harmonious perfection acts in, as and through me, precisely as I am in the moment.

I deeply know that the action of this harmonious perfection is the sole operating force in the Universe.

I radically rely on this harmonious perfection to support every moment of my human experience.

I unconditionally experience and express the harmonious perfection of the Universe in every activity of my life.

I exalt in the joyful abundance richly invested in me by the harmonious perfection of the Universe.

And, I gleefully exalt in the extravaganza of unconditional love and support that constantly and consistently surrounds me, and all in the Universe.

THE HUMAN EXPERIENCE

The human experience is but an exercise for the Soul to practice Its perfection. It is not a trivial experience, and many a Soul return to it time and again to master the challenges it offers.

You are that Soul, returned to the human, to practice the perfection of who you truly are. You are that Soul, deeply engrossed in the human, so that your mastery is complete. You are seeing that now.

You are seeing that the events of the human have no real meaning, other than to allow you to experience and accept your mastery. The deep emotional chasms of the human but afford you the opportunity of the deep knowing of your Self. You are seeing that getting involved in the drama of the human events is but the challenge to your Soul Self to remember who you are and why you chose this experience.

We have long shared with each other the concept of human perfection—that it's all perfect, just the way it is. And, the truth of that is evidenced in the creative and magnificent activities you create to practice and experience the reality of your true Self. Let's look at a few:

The Body

In the human, the body represents the identity of an individual, as well as the evidence of its life. No body—no life. You see that this opportunity affords you, the Soul, to experience and practice your eternal manifestation of the infinitely unfolding nature of God, your Source. Body size or shape is but a reminder of the formless, powerful energy you are. In the human, you create "norms" or "ideals" around shape and form. Again, what a beautiful and perfect opportunity to express and experience the infinite originality of Self. In the depiction of your creation by God, there is only the recitation of you being made in "God's image" and "Behold, it was very good." In the human, the practice is to look to the manifestation to see what God is like. The practice of the Soul is to look to God to know what the creation truly is.

Financial Affairs

This is one you truly enjoy playing with. In the human, you have adopted what you call "a money-driven society." It takes money to do almost anything, and you have made money a condition for having or experiencing any sense of comfort, security or enjoyment. What a perfect opportunity for the Soul to experience true unconditional love and support. You have always seen a lack of money as somehow a failure on your part to succeed—that you must do something, even in consciousness, to allow money to be a part of your experience.

The activity around money is one of the most supportive activities the Soul has in experiencing and expressing Its perfection. One of the most entrenched beliefs set up in the human is that you cannot live without money. And, you have many on the planet acting out that belief. Even more entrenched is the belief that you can solve these peoples' problems with money. I have been attributed as the source of the statement "the poor will always be with you." Well, they will, as long as there is a Soul in the human practicing Its acceptance of full and total abundance. I have said to you, "Money is in total support of you," and it is. Acknowledging, accepting and appreciating your financial affairs, just as they are, opens you to the support of money. Loving, unconditionally, not having money is the activity the Soul creates for It Self. You are that Soul. Your commitment to receive and enjoy bountiful financial abundance is a commitment to loving your current financial abundance just the way it is. You will experience huge amounts of money in your life when money is no longer a condition in your life.

You are seeing this; you, as the perfect Soul in the human, are embracing, in deep love and appreciation, all aspects of your financial affairs just as they are. The wealth encountered in that experience is beyond money.

Relationships

Whether you are relating to your family, a spouse, a lover, a pet, the grocery clerk, your relationships provide the Soul with a wealth of perfect opportunities to practice Its wholeness and completeness. In the human, a "perfect" relationship is revered as a blessing and an accomplishment. The Soul accepts any and all relationships as perfect precisely as they are. The Soul views all relationships as supportive and utilizes the activity of them to practice Its perfection. The Soul knows that the perfect relationship is the one It has with Its Source, and It knows that that relationship is infinite, unconditionally loving and supportive. You are that Soul.

We began this meditation on the perfection of the human ex-perience and the support it is constantly and consistently offering you, the perfect Soul. Acknowledge, accept and appreciate each and every activity of your human experience just as it is. It will not change itself, nor allow you to change it. It will remain precisely as it is to give you the opportunity to do what you came here to do—*love it all.*

THE BUSINESS OF BEING

You have asked me to speak to you about "business." In the beginning humans came together to support their existence upon the planet. Gradually as each began to develop and enjoy certain aspects and talents, the joy of contribution to the whole was experienced and ex-pressed. Then, contribution began to be valued on "better" and "more," and "needless" and "not enough." Thus, when one made a contribu-tion to the whole, another sought to make a "better" contribution—and all began to be judged on the quality of their contributions. This activity of rejecting some contribution in favor of others (you now call this business) evolved into the judgment that permeates the collective consciousness today. So, what is judgment? It is unrequited love—love offered but not accepted.

I wish to remind you that all Souls come to the human experience to play. It is like a game of hide and seek. In order to come to the hu-man, the Soul must hide its omnipotence, omniscience and its abil-ity to unconditionally, non-judgmentally accept and love everything just the way it is. In order to "be" human, the Soul hides It Self in its human experiences. Then, with inexhaustible and unerring support from the Universe, this human begins to seek its Soul. It knows where to look—in the human experiences where it was hidden in the first place.

Each of us chose certain human events and conditions to experience.

We made this choice long before we came here. We chose those who would support us in hiding our Soul, and those who would support us in finding it. We carefully outlined the support we wanted from the Universe.

Now, we are at the "seek" part of the game. We look for our non-judgmental, all-powerful, all-knowing, all-accepting Self. Yet hiding and seeking is not all there is to the game. Remember, when found, there is the race back to home base where we are either "Free" or "It". (That's how I remember the game being played.) And, so it is in our game. When we begin to find our Soulness—our power to love and accept under all conditions and circumstances—we have the opportunity to move our consciousness again to our "home base," our complete and total awareness of the perfection of all things. We don't die to do this. We live to do it. And, the steps in seeking, finding, and returning to home base are all the same—loving and accepting every event and circumstance in our daily lives just the way they are.

It is the same in the game of business. You look attentively at all those things that you would "change," and you love them, you accept them, you unlock the judgment from around them! As your loving energy meets with the energy of the judgment, there is a fusion of power so beatific that it is felt by everyone and everything in the Universe.

Remember, you're not seeking to overcome judgment. You are finding it to love it, to accept it, to blend your power of unconditional love with its own power of unrequited love, in order to establish in consciousness a home base (a business if you will) of total love and support.

That, my precious one, is the free enterprise system.

SEPTEMBER 27, 2001

What an opportunity to practice our spiritual knowing! We are clear that every event in our human experience is a mirror of our own consciousness. We are clear that we create these events to give ourselves the opportunity to look at any limited beliefs we may still be holding in order to open them up to a broader and more expansive view of our true selves.

So, in light of current events, we ask: "How are we terrorizing ourselves?"; "What do we believe is 'outside' ourselves to terrorize us?"; and "How can I be a victim and of whom?"

Webster defines "terror" as "a state of intense fear." If we witnessed what went on in New York, and subsequent events, we can be sure that we hold this limited belief in consciousness in some manner or form. We are still holding the belief that there is an outside force or power that can victimize us.

Now, these events were not created to be fixed. They were not created to be avenged or acted upon in any way. They were created for the sole purpose of giving each of us the opportunity to expand our consciousness of who we truly are. And, who are we? The Power and Presence of God, right here, right now, experiencing and expressing as our Selves. That is the absolute truth about every living thing in the Universe.

My Guidance tells me that "terror" is a clever disguise that I created to hide the intense unconditional love and trust that is the essence of my Soul being, so that this Soul could play in the human as me. He tells me that in order to play in the human my Soul disguised It Self in limited beliefs so that it could have the fun of first experiencing these beliefs, then of unraveling the disguises to reveal It Self once again. I totally trust my Guidance and believe that we all have given ourselves the opportunity to experience the human from our Soul's awareness.

As we fill our consciousness with the absolute truth of the unconditional love, trust, abundance, beauty, harmony, joy of who we truly are, that is what we experience. As we see the events of our day as the opportunity to expand our awareness and experience of these truths, we appreciate and value these events as gifts from the Universe. As we open to receive these gifts, without judgment, our acceptance deepens our trust of our true Selfhood. I support my Self and each one of you in enthusiastically and exuberantly embracing these opportunities.

Lightning Source UK Ltd.
Milton Keynes UK
UKOW04f0401081215

264260UK00001B/187/P